It Happened In Seri

IT HAPPENED IN MONTANA

SECOND EDITION

James A. Crutchfield

TWODOT®

GUILFORD, CONNECTICUT
HELENA, MONTANA
AN IMPRINT OF THE GLOBE PEQUOT PRESS

The publisher gratefully acknowledges the assistance of Dr. William J. Furdell, Department of History, College of Great Falls.

A · TWODOT® · BOOK

Text design by Nancy Freeborn
Map by M. A. Dubé © 2008 Morris Book Publishing, LLC
Front cover photo: Piegan tepees, ca. 1910. Library of Congress, LC-USZ62-101262
Back cover photo: Columbia Gardens, Butte, Montana, courtesy of the Library of Congress

Library of Congress Cataloging-in-Publication Data
Crutchfield, James Andrew, 1938-
It happened in Montana / James A. Crutchfield.—2nd Globe Pequot ed.
p. cm.
ISBN-13: 978-0-7627-4568-5
ISBN-10: 0-7627-4568-1
1. Montana—History—Anecdotes. 2. Montana—Biography—Anecdotes. I. Title.
F731.6.C78 2007
978.6—dc22
2007026023

Manufactured in the United States of America
Second Edition/Third Printing

To Regena, for our happy days together in Montana,
and to Bob S., who made it all possible.

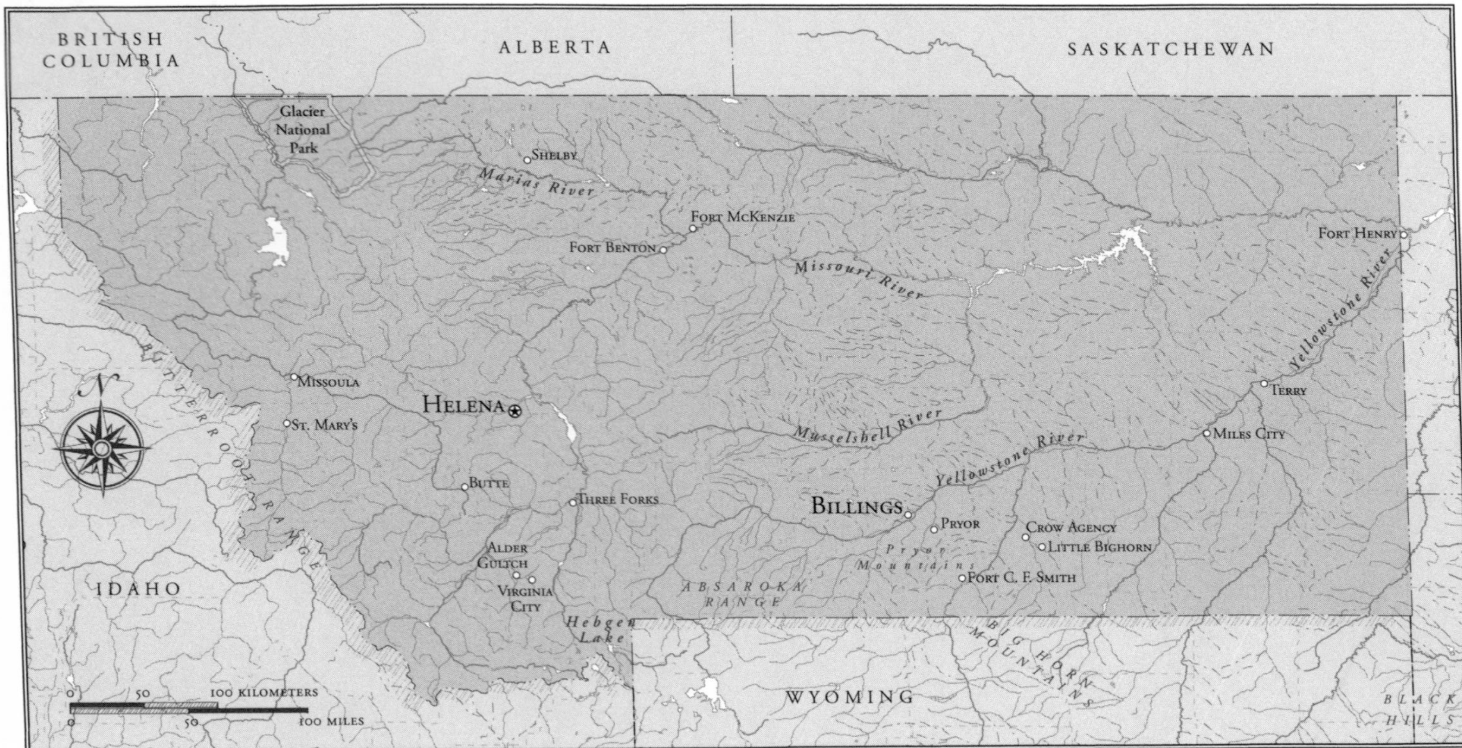
BRITISH COLUMBIA
ALBERTA
SASKATCHEWAN
Glacier National Park
SHELBY
Marias River
FORT MCKENZIE
FORT BENTON
Missouri River
FORT HENRY
Yellowstone River
TERRY
MILES CITY
MISSOULA
HELENA
ST. MARY'S
BITTERROOT RANGE
Musselshell River
Yellowstone River
BUTTE
THREE FORKS
BILLINGS
PRYOR
CROW AGENCY
LITTLE BIGHORN
Pryor Mountains
FORT C. F. SMITH
ALDER GULCH
VIRGINIA CITY
IDAHO
ABSAROKA RANGE
Hebgen Lake
BIG HORN MOUNTAINS
WYOMING
BLACK HILLS
0 50 100 KILOMETERS
0 50 100 MILES

MONTANA

CONTENTS

PREFACE

This book highlights several fascinating episodes of Montana history, beginning with the first recorded visit to the area by white men in the mid-eighteenth century and continuing through to the present. Each story is complete in and of itself and may be read individually and out of sequence.

Although these vignettes don't in any way purport to be a thorough history of the state, they've been selected to give the reader a broad understanding of the historical background of "Big Sky Country."

I hope that *It Happened in Montana* will provide a few hours of pleasure to those who read it and that it will, perhaps, find its way into the classrooms of the state, thereby giving younger generations a better appreciation of their vast heritage.

A FIRST GLIMPSE OF THE SHINING MOUNTAINS

- 1743 -

The four Frenchmen and their Indian companions narrowed their eyes to search the western horizon. The frigid January wind blew directly into their faces as they sat astride their horses on a small knoll in what may now be southeastern Montana.

One of the Frenchmen suddenly became excited and, arms waving, pointed out a vast outcropping of stone in the distance. The range of snowcapped peaks looked more like wispy clouds than mountains until the men left their vantage point and rode several miles closer.

Long before Thomas Jefferson dreamed of finding a northwest passage from the United States to the Pacific Ocean, French authorities in Canada had the same vision. As early as 1673 Marquette and Joliet explored the Mississippi River valley; the great La Salle followed in their footsteps a few years later. More than half a century would pass before intrepid fur traders from Canada would venture beyond the "father of waters" and cross the Great Plains.

In 1732 a distinguished French fur trader with the formidable name of Pierre Gaultier de Varennes, Sieur de la Verendrye, established a trading post in present-day Lake of the Woods County, Minnesota. The Frenchman used the post as a base for further exploration to the west. By 1738 Verendrye had traveled across the plains as far as present-day North Dakota, where he visited among the Mandan Indians.

Verendrye was enthralled by the stories the Mandans told him. Far to the west, they said, was a great lake whose salty waters rose and fell at regular intervals. The elders of the tribe also described white men with long beards who worshipped in houses built especially for that purpose and who read books and sang strange songs. Verendrye immediately concluded that the Spanish already had possession of the Pacific coast.

The aging Verendrye hurried home to Montreal and pleaded with authorities there to finance yet another attempt to find the mythical passage to the Pacific Ocean. But French influence in the New World was waning, and more important matters occupied the leadership than Indian tales about a route to the Pacific that years of active exploration had failed to discover.

It wasn't until 1742 that Verendrye was able to muster enough support for his expedition. But poor health forced the Frenchman to turn its leadership over to his two sons, Louis-Joseph and Francois. The old man watched as his progeny and two other countrymen turned their heads to the west, and he silently prayed that his sons would have the persistence and luck to locate the passage that he had spent much of his life attempting to find.

The two brothers set out for the Mandan villages and beyond, encountering several other Indian tribes along the way. None could shed further light on the elusive passage to the Pacific Ocean. When the Verendryes reached the encampment of a tribe they called the"Bows," the brothers found that the Indians were preparing to go to war against the Shoshones, who lived a number of miles to the west. The Verendryes decided to travel with the Bow war party, hoping they might encounter other Indians who could tell them something definitive about the route to the west coast.

On January 1, 1743, the Verendryes and their companions spotted a mountain chain far to the west. These "Shining Mountains," as they called them, were probably the Bighorn Range, which spans the border between Montana and Wyoming. If so, the brothers had probably crossed into southeastern Montana—the first white men recorded to have done so.

The massive mountains blocking their way, the Verendryes turned their horses homeward. Although no one knows for sure whether they were the first Europeans to visit "Big Sky Country," they did at least find the eastern fringes of the Rockies, which stood in the way of the passage they sought.

LEWIS'S CONFRONTATION WITH THE BLACKFEET

- 1806 -

ALMOST TWO HUNDRED YEARS AFTER Meriwether Lewis killed a Blackfoot Indian in Montana, scholars still debate whether the incident was responsible for the tribe's fanatical hostility toward white men for years to come. Certainly the tribe was a force to be reckoned with by frontiersmen for decades after the Lewis and Clark Expedition passed through Blackfeet territory in 1806.

Throughout their trip Lewis and Clark suffered from heat, cold, wet, illness, hunger, and thirst, but they had remarkable luck in their dealings with the various Indian tribes they met. That all changed in the summer of 1806, as the expedition headed back to St. Louis after reaching the Pacific Ocean.

At Traveler's Rest, near the site of present-day Missoula, Lewis and Clark decided to split their command in order to explore more territory. On July 3, 1806, Lewis took a small party and headed down the Bitterroot River and then northeastward toward the Great Falls of the Missouri. Clark and the rest of the men set out toward the Three Forks of the Missouri. The two parties were to rendezvous about five weeks later near the confluence of the Yellowstone and Missouri Rivers.

Lewis's main goals were to pick up supplies and specimens the expedition had cached near the Great Falls and to explore the Marias River, a stream that flowed into the Missouri from the north. Leaving some of his men to move boats and equipment around the Great Falls, he and three others—George Drouillard and Joseph and Reuben Field—went on to explore the Marias.

On July 18 Lewis's small party reached the Marias River and spent the next several days exploring the stream's sources. The weather turned nasty, and after spending several days in the rain and cold, a dejected Lewis decided it was time to head back downstream to meet the others. Before leaving camp he christened it Camp Disappointment.

On July 26 Lewis saw a band of eight Indians observing his party from a distance. Uncertain which tribe the Indians represented, he decided to "advance towards them in a friendly manner," he later reported in his journal.

The Indians turned out to be Piegans, a branch of the Blackfeet. After much shaking of hands and many salutations, the two groups pitched camp together, but Lewis was wary of the Piegans and told his men to be on the lookout in case they tried to steal the horses.

Lewis described in his journal what happened next:

> *At sunrise the Indians got up and crowded round the fire near which J. Fields, who was then on watch, had carelessly left his rifle, near the head of his brother, who was still asleep. One of the Indians slipped behind him,*

and unperceived [sic], took his brother's and his own rifle, while at the same time, two others seized those of Drewyer and captain Lewis.

In the ensuing scuffle Reuben Fields stabbed one Indian, killing the brave instantly. Lewis fired his pistol at a retreating Piegan and hit him in the stomach. The Indian later died. The other six Piegans fled, and Lewis called for his men to do the same, since he didn't know how many of the Indians' cohorts might be nearby.

The four explorers rode southward at a hectic pace, covering nearly 120 miles in the next twenty-four hours. Only when they reached the Missouri and met up with the party from the Great Falls did they feel they were out of danger. The men continued downstream to their rendezvous with Clark.

Later, Lewis must have thought often of this incident. During the entire expedition—one that had taken twenty-eight months and had carried its members more than 8,000 miles through uncharted wilderness—the affair with the Blackfeet was the only significant difficulty with Indians. It was unfortunate that the skirmish cast a pall over the last few weeks of an otherwise highly successful expedition.

JOHN COLTER'S SPRINT FOR LIFE

- 1808 -

JOHN COLTER FELT LIKE HE HAD BEEN RUNNING FOR DAYS. His heart pounded against his ribs as he forced his legs to carry him faster, faster, faster. He rubbed his sweaty face and then glanced at his hand. Blood! His nose was bleeding! His head felt like it would burst!

Colter kept running as fast as he could but managed to look over his shoulder. The Indians were still after him, although there weren't as many as there had been a few minutes ago. If he could just get rid of that one brave who was closing in on him, he might make it.

Glancing over his shoulder again, Colter quickly formulated a plan. When the rapidly approaching Indian got to within a few yards of him, Colter stopped abruptly and turned. The brave, taken by surprise, stumbled and started to fall but managed to thrust his lance at the white man. Colter stepped aside, and the lance point broke off as it struck the ground. He retrieved it and stabbed the Indian. Within seconds Colter had resumed his steady pace, leaving the dying brave behind.

Only three or four braves pursued him now, and they were several hundred yards behind. For the first time Colter may have thought he would survive this ordeal. As he sprinted through the cacti and rough prairie grasses, he may have considered just how he'd ended up in this predicament to begin with.

Colter had been a member of the Lewis and Clark Expedition. On the return trip from the Pacific Ocean to St. Louis in 1806, the party had met two trappers who were heading westward into the Rocky Mountains to trap beaver. They asked Colter if he would like to accompany them, and after conferring with Lewis and Clark and obtaining their blessing, he agreed to guide the pair back into the mountains.

The fate of the two trappers is unknown, but by the spring of 1807, Colter had returned to the Mandan villages on the Missouri River. There he met Manuel Lisa and his party of trappers, who were also headed for the upper Missouri River country. Again, Colter threw in his lot with the trappers and guided them to the confluence of the Bighorn and Yellowstone Rivers, where Lisa built a fur-trading post.

Impressed with Colter, Lisa sent him on a mission to inform the various Indian tribes in the region that Lisa was hoping to trade with them for furs. Colter successfully met the Crows, with whom he became fast friends. It was also during this journey that he's credited with discovering what is today Yellowstone National Park and what has become known as "Colter's Hell" on the Shoshone River near Cody, Wyoming.

In the fall of 1808, Colter set out to trap the Jefferson River with a companion, John Potts. One day, they were confronted by many Blackfeet warriors who ordered them to drop their weapons. Potts impetuously shot a brave and was instantly riddled with arrows. Colter was captured, stripped naked, and carried before the elders of the tribe.

One chief asked Colter if he could run fast, and John replied that he couldn't. He correctly guessed that the chief was considering letting him run for his life. The Indians gave him a head start of a few hundred yards and then quickly gave chase. Colter broke into a run and was immediately followed by several Blackfeet warriors, no doubt the fastest the tribe had to offer.

Colter headed for the Madison Fork (or the Jefferson, depending upon which account one believes), hoping he could cross the six miles of prairie to the river and escape his enemies. As he came within a few hundred yards of the river, he peered over his shoulder and saw that the closest of his pursuers was still far behind. He jumped into the icy waters and hid under a pile of driftwood.

Soon the panting braves appeared and scoured the riverbanks for any sign of the vanished white man. For hours Colter lay in the frigid waters beneath the brush, waiting for dark and then dawn. By the next morning, the Blackfeet had given up their search, and Colter pulled his frozen body from the stream. He had survived the Indians, but now he must travel—naked, barefoot, freezing, and starving—to Fort Lisa, a distance of 250 miles.

Eleven days later, Colter literally fell through the gates at the fort, much to the amazement of his friends and associates there. They couldn't believe their eyes at the sight of his emaciated, haggard form. And they didn't know whether to believe his tale. Colter didn't care. Less than two years later, he left the Rocky Mountains, never to return to the wilderness he loved. He died of jaundice on a Missouri farm at the age of thirty-nine.

THE BIRTH AND DEATH OF A FUR COMPANY

- 1823 -

For many years the upper Missouri River valley and the eastern front of the Rocky Mountains were hotbeds of activity for the American fur trade. Hundreds of self-styled "mountain men" traipsed the rough terrain of the Missouri watershed, searching for beaver, whose fur was popularly used to make gentlemen's hats.

When Lewis and Clark returned to St. Louis in 1806, their stories of the primitive, wildlife-rich mountains of the West fell on fertile ears among some of the businessmen there. One of these men, Manuel Lisa, a Louisiana Spaniard by birth, was quick to follow up on what he thought was a sure way to make his fortune. In 1807 Lisa traveled upriver as far as the confluence of the Bighorn and Yellowstone Rivers, where his men built Fort Lisa, or Manuel's Fort, as it was sometimes called. This was the first permanent structure erected by white men in Montana.

Lisa returned to St. Louis in 1808 and, the next year, organized the Missouri Fur Company, with which he hoped to monopolize the upper Missouri fur trade. For the next several years, he sent many expeditions up the "Big Muddy." The Missouri Fur Company's coffers alternated between full and empty as it vigorously pursued its fickle business.

Despite the moderate success of Lisa's company, it had its problems. For one thing the organization was made up of many of the leading citizens of St. Louis, and even though Lisa was in control of daily operations, it was difficult to conduct business with so many "chiefs." Secondly, the Blackfeet Indians, with whom Lisa desperately wanted to trade, were hostile to white men, and the fur company was unable to make peaceful contact with them. Fort Lisa had to be deserted in 1811 because of futile attempts to deal with the adamant Blackfeet. Lisa moved his main theater of operations down the Missouri and established new headquarters at Council Bluffs, in what is today Nebraska.

Over the years the Missouri Fur Company reorganized several times until finally, in 1819, Lisa was appointed its president. He was the only one of the original organizers to remain active in the company, but his success was short lived. On August 12, 1820, Manuel Lisa died of illness in St. Louis.

Joshua Pilcher, a protege of Lisa, took over the day-to-day management of the company. Immediately, Pilcher reopened the upriver trade, and in the fall of 1821, at the site of the old Fort Lisa, he built a new structure, which he called Fort Benton. The company thrived under Pilcher and in 1822 shipped $25,000 worth of furs downriver to St. Louis. With three hundred men in the field, the Missouri Fur Company appeared to be on the way to the success that eluded its founder.

Then the Blackfeet menace resurfaced. In the spring of 1823, Pilcher sent two trappers, Robert Jones and Michael Immel, along with twenty-eight companions, into the Three Forks area, hoping to establish peaceful contact with the Blackfeet. Pilcher instructed Jones and Immel to "use every effort to obtain a friendly interview with the Blackfoot Indians, and to incur any reasonable expense for the accomplishment of that object; and to impress them with the friendly disposition of American citizens towards them. . . ."

In May, Jones and Immel met a party of Blackfeet along the Jefferson River. The two groups exchanged pleasantries, and the Blackfeet seemed to warm to the idea of having trading posts in the area. The following morning, the Indians left in a peaceable mood.

Unsure of the sincerity of the Blackfeet, Jones and Immel left the area immediately, following the Yellowstone River to a spot near the site of present-day Billings. Suddenly, Blackfeet warriors exploded from the rimrock. In a matter of minutes, Jones, Immel, and five of their followers were killed. The Indians took all of the trappers' property, including thirty-five packs of beaver, horses, and traps, all worth about $15,000.

The Missouri Fur Company had been dealt its final blow. Pilcher wrote, "The flower of my business is gone; my mountaineers have been defeated, and the chiefs of the party both slain."

Pilcher ran the company for several more years but on a much smaller scale. Finally, two of its largest competitors, the American Fur Company and the Rocky Mountain Fur Company, squeezed it completely out of business. So ended the first American attempts to establish a fur trade in the shadow of the northern Rockies.

MIKE FINK:
A ROWDY AT HENRY'S FORT

- 1823 -

Mike Fink was a rowdy, no doubt about it. By 1823 his reputation had spread up and down the Missouri River, from St. Louis to Henry's Fort at the mouth of the Yellowstone River. He was known as a bully and a brutal, deadly fighter.

Fink was born around 1770 near Pittsburgh. He grew to manhood at the edge of the frontier and as a boy learned the ways of the mighty Ohio River. He eventually became a master flatboatman.

Fink quickly became renowned throughout the Ohio and Mississippi river valleys. There were few saloons between Pittsburgh and New Orleans that he hadn't frequented and few men who hadn't heard of his prowess as a troublemaker.

Not a large man by today's standards—he stood about five feet, nine inches tall and weighed 180 pounds—he was often in trouble. For example, in St. Louis in 1821, he shot a black man in the heel "so he could wear a genteel boot," according to the *Missouri Intelligencer.*

Perhaps this escapade and the wild rumors that circulated about him caused Fink to sign up with General William Ashley's first fur-trading expedition up the Missouri River in 1822. Accompanied by two close friends, William Carpenter and Levi Talbot, Fink made his way up the "Big Muddy" with a party led by Ashley's associate, Major Andrew Henry.

By the fall of 1822, the group had reached the mouth of the Yellowstone River. There, Major Henry and his men constructed a small fort, appropriately named Henry's Fort or Fort Henry. From the fort teams of men spread out along the streams and rivers in the region to trap beaver. Fink, Carpenter, and Talbot headed west and established an encampment at the mouth of the Musselshell River. They decided to spend the winter there and return to Henry's Fort the following spring.

No one knows what transpired among the three friends that winter on the Musselshell. Perhaps the bitter cold and the loneliness of the long nights got the best of them. Legend says that Fink and Carpenter got into a feud over an Indian woman, but no tribes were in the area at the time. Whatever the reason, the two men feuded.

As spring melted the snow around the encampment, it also seemed to dispel the bad blood between Fink and Carpenter. When they started back to Henry's Fort, they appeared to be the best of friends. Somewhere along the way, tempers flared once more, but by the time they reached the fort, all was calm again.

Once at the fort, where whiskey flowed freely, Fink suggested that he and Carpenter solidify their renewed friendship by playing a game they'd played often in the past. The object of the game was to shoot a tin cup full of whiskey from the other participant's head.

Carpenter cautiously agreed, a coin was flipped, and Fink won the toss. While Carpenter nervously balanced the cup on his head, Fink counted off sixty paces. Sensing that Fink hadn't truly forgiven him, Carpenter had earlier told Talbot that he expected Fink to shoot him dead. He wanted Talbot to have all his possessions.

Fink and Carpenter faced each other on the prairie outside Henry's Fort. The news had spread throughout the compound, and practically all of Ashley's men were gathered around to watch.

"Hold your noodle steady, Carpenter, and don't spill the whiskey, as I shall want some presently," shouted Fink as he slowly drew a bead on the tiny cup atop Carpenter's head.

The flintlock rifle spoke, and everyone watched in amazement as Carpenter, a bloody hole in the center of his forehead, dropped dead to the ground.

"Carpenter, you have spilled the whiskey," exclaimed Fink as he calmly strode off to the fort.

Although Fink denied shooting Carpenter on purpose, Talbot knew that his associate was guilty of outright murder. A few weeks later, when Fink was in a drunken stupor, he admitted that he'd killed Carpenter.

"I shot him like I would a dog!" he boasted.

At that, Talbot drew the very pistol that Carpenter had left him and shot Fink, killing him instantly.

Talbot wasn't charged with murder. In fact, most of the men at the fort thought that Fink deserved his fate and were happy the troublemaker was gone. Sometime later, after taking part in Colonel Henry Leavenworth's attempts to subdue the Arikara Indian villages along the Missouri River, Talbot drowned in the Teton River while attempting to swim across it.

And so ends the story of three friends who were as wild and unpredictable as the mighty Montana wilderness they shared.

PRINCE MAXIMILIAN: TOURIST ROYALE

- 1833 -

On April 10, 1833, along the muddy banks of the Missouri River at St. Louis, the steamboat *Yellowstone* prepared to leave for the American Fur Company's upriver trading posts. Among the one hundred or so passengers—mostly deckhands, trappers, and French *engages*—were three distinguished European guests who had come to America to explore the upper Missouri River and study the region's Indian tribes.

The leader of the foreign expedition was a fifty-year-old German named Alexander Philipp Maximilian, Prince zu Wied. With him was Swiss-born artist Karl Bodmer, age twenty-four, and a family retainer named David Dreidoppel, age unknown.

Maximilian was a naturalist who had already gained a reputation as an ethnologist during earlier Brazilian explorations. Now he wanted to capture in text and paintings the Plains Indians in their natural environment, much as the American artist George Catlin had just done.

On June 24 the *Yellowstone* and its illustrious passengers arrived at Fort Union, at the confluence of the Yellowstone and Missouri Rivers. The steamer had traveled eighteen hundred miles upstream in about two and a half months. For almost two weeks Maximilian and his two companions stayed at Fort Union. The prince busied himself describing the fort and its Indian neighbors, Bodmer painted landscapes and Indians with a passion, and Dreidoppel collected wildlife specimens. Finally, Maximilian decided it was time to move on to his final destination, the Rocky Mountains. On the morning of July 6, the three Europeans boarded a keelboat named *Flora,* which powered by seven strong French *engages,* headed up the Missouri to Fort McKenzie, near the mouth of the Marias River.

For the next 650 miles, the group passed through some of Montana's most beautiful country, and, after thirty-four days, they approached Fort McKenzie, deep in the heart of Blackfeet country. Maximilian wrote the following about this hostile tribe:

> *They are always dangerous to white men who are hunting singly in the mountains, especially to beaver hunters, and kill them whenever they fall into their hands; hence the armed troops of the traders keep up a constant war with them. It was said that in the year 1832, they shot fifty-eight Whites and, a couple of years before that time, above eighty.*

Maximilian witnessed an unusual Blackfeet custom while at Fort McKenzie. In his journal for August 15, 1833, he wrote:

> *In the evening, we went to the tents of the Indians where we saw at least six women whose noses had been*

cut off. This is the way in which the Piegans and other Blackfeet punish the infidelity of their women, a hideous disfigurement.

The three also witnessed a fierce battle between a band of friendly Blackfeet, who had a small camp outside the stockade, and a larger group of Assiniboines and Crees. Bodmer quickly sketched the action and consequently became the first white artist ever to capture on paper an Indian battle he personally observed.

Prince Maximilian and his men finally departed Fort McKenzie, arriving in the Mandan country on November 8. They never returned to Montana, but their descriptions and paintings reveal what the state was like to its first "tourists."

FATHER DESMET'S CHAPEL IN THE PINES

- 1841 -

FATHER PIERRE-JEAN DESMET WAS AS HAPPY AS he'd ever been in his life. On that memorable day in 1838, the Belgian-born priest learned he was being sent to the villages of the Potawatomi Indians, near the site of present-day Council Bluffs, Iowa. His mission was to spread the gospel among the Indians, a dream the thirty-seven-year-old man of God had nurtured since arriving in America years before.

Father DeSmet was twenty years old when he came to the United States. He settled near Baltimore, but two years later moved to the vicinity of St. Louis, Missouri. In 1827 he was ordained a priest in the Jesuit order of the Catholic Church.

DeSmet taught at the University of St. Louis for several years and then traveled to Europe for an extended stay. Throughout this time he aspired to a ministry with the Indians, and now, among the Potawatomis, he finally had his chance.

But fate had something different in store for Father DeSmet. As he happily went about his job among the Potawatomis, he met a delegation of Flathead Indians who had traveled east from their homes at the headwaters of the Missouri River. DeSmet learned this was the last of four delegations that had come downstream in recent years hoping to persuade some religious organization to come among their people and teach them Christianity.

Rushing home to St. Louis, DeSmet informed his superiors of his conversations with the Flatheads. He urged church officials to let him travel to their remote country and establish a mission there. Knowing the church's goal of converting as many natives as possible, DeSmet assumed correctly that permission would be granted.

In the spring of 1840, DeSmet set out from Westport, Missouri, with the American Fur Company's annual caravan. With the party were the renowned mountain men Jim Bridger and Henry Fraeb. DeSmet had accumulated four horses and three mules for the trip, and he was accompanied by several other men.

As the group crossed Kansas, Father DeSmet wrote in his journal:

> *Until the 17th of May we traveled westward over immense plains, destitute of trees or shrubs, except along the streams, and broken by deep ravines, where our voyageurs lowered and raised the carts by means of ropes . . . often the thermometer would be as low as 27 in the morning, though it might rise to 90 by noon.*

Father DeSmet traveled with the fur caravan as far as the rendezvous site on the Green River, in what is today Wyoming. From there he proceeded with a Flathead escort to Pierre's Hole, where several hundred more Indians met him. DeSmet parleyed with the

Flatheads for about two months, using the time to scout the surrounding countryside for a mission site. He entered what is now Montana, visiting the Three Forks area as well as the surrounding mountains. Returning to St. Louis that summer, DeSmet made plans to come back the following year and establish his mission.

In May 1841 the priest was aboard an emigrant train traveling the Oregon Trail to Fort Hall in what is now Idaho. When he arrived at the fort, he was again met by his Flathead friends and escorted to their villages. There in the Bitterroot Valley, about thirty miles south of present-day Missoula, the kindly priest established St. Mary's Mission, the first church in what was to become Montana.

DeSmet introduced the Flatheads to the advantages of farming at the same time as he spread the Gospel. Potatoes, oats, and wheat were planted in the spring of 1842 and in the fall became the first domestic crops harvested in Montana.

By 1850 younger generations of Indians had shown dwindling interest in religion. They may also have been angered by Father DeSmet's attempts to take religion to their enemies, the Blackfeet. Relations became so bad that the mission closed its doors. But by then Father DeSmet was gone, spreading the Word among other remote Indian tribes in the Northwest.

Major John Owen bought St. Mary's Mission in 1850 and converted the buildings to a fort appropriately called Fort Owen. The fort was used for many years as a supply point for trappers, fur traders, farmers, and stagecoach drivers. When Owen discovered gold near the place in 1852, there was a flurry of new activity.

Eventually, hostile Blackfeet forced Owen to abandon his fort, but its buildings and those of St. Mary's lingered in the shadow of the Bitterroot Mountains for years to come, a reminder of the early days of the Catholic Church in Montana.

LIVER-EATING JOHNSTON'S GRUESOME REVENGE

- 1843 -

When he arrived in St. Joseph, Missouri, in 1843, John Johnston had no idea he would become a legend in his own time. Not quite twenty years old, Johnston was already a giant among men. Some say he was over six feet tall and weighed close to two hundred pounds. Born in New Jersey, Johnston had never before set foot west of the Mississippi River. Still, he had been around. According to one report, he had worked on a whaling ship for a time.

Johnston was intent on becoming a mountain man. He had heard endless stories back home of the wilderness that lay up the Missouri River, and he wanted to become part of it before it disappeared. When he arrived in Missouri, he was on his way to the Rocky Mountains to trap beaver and see the vast homeland of the American Indian.

As Johnston shopped for supplies in St. Joseph, it was obvious he was a greenhorn. Browsing from counter to counter, Johnston finally purchased a Hawken rifle, a Bowie knife, and a tomahawk to take to the mountains. He also bought a horse to carry him and his supplies across the plains. Then Johnston pointed himself toward the "Shining Mountains" and into the folklore of America.

Johnston served his apprenticeship in the mountains under such men as John Hatcher and Old Bill Williams, both experienced fur trappers. Some authorities believe Johnston left the mountains for a brief period during the Mexican War to serve in the U.S. Navy. This seems doubtful, since he picked a fine day in May 1847—right in the middle of America's conflict with Mexico—to marry a Flathead Indian girl.

His bride's Indian name meant "the swan," and she was as graceful and beautiful as the wild, white birds that flew over the mountains every fall on their way south. Johnston paid dearly for her. He gave her father, Bear's Head, one rifle, two knives, and several pounds each of salt and sugar, in addition to gifts he distributed to the girl's immediate family.

Johnston took his new wife back to a cabin he had built on the Little Snake River, probably in what is Idaho today. For a few weeks he enjoyed the rewards of marriage. But beaver season was coming soon, and Johnston knew he had to leave his bride and head for the icy streams that poured out of the mountains. He had to trap the rich furs that would pay for next year's supplies. Making certain to leave The Swan well-provisioned, he bid her farewell.

Johnston was horribly surprised when he returned home from his trapping expedition. As he approached his cabin, he immediately sensed that something was wrong. For a long time he studied the area from a distance, and when he was satisfied that there was no danger, he proceeded into the forest opening that contained his home. There, he discovered the stark, white skull of The Swan, and not far away lay the rest of her skeleton. Mixed in with her bones were the tiny skull and skeleton of a human fetus. Johnston turned away as he wondered whether his wife would have borne him a son or a daughter.

The angry mountain man pieced together what had happened as best he could from the signs around the cabin. A Crow war party had definitely killed and scalped his wife and smothered the life of his unborn child. And it didn't take long to find that the Indians had ransacked his cabin and taken practically everything of value.

Johnston carefully placed the skeletal remains of his wife and child in an iron kettle, which he carried to a secret place in the forest. He placed the pot in a deep crevice in the side of a cliff, and as far as anyone knows, there it still remains.

Johnston made a pact with himself that day. He would never meet another Crow who would not pay with his life for the murder of his family. He became the archenemy of the entire Crow nation, and his prowess and effectiveness at killing young braves became rapidly known throughout the native population.

One after another Crow warrior paid dearly for the war party's attack that day on the Little Snake. Horrified survivors observed that Johnston would cut open the bellies of his victims, extract their livers, and rub the blood from these organs into his long beard. And so the legend of "Liver-Eating" Johnston was born.

At one point the Crows sent out twenty handpicked warriors to track down and kill Johnston. But instead, the mountain man managed to kill every one of his would-be assassins. Johnston gained such a reputation among Indians and whites alike that mothers in the settlements would sometimes threaten their naughty children with "I'm going to get Liver-Eating Johnston after you!"

Eventually, Johnston tired of all the killing. He strode into a Crow village one day and declared that his bloody vendetta was over. The Crows respected him for his prowess and bravery, and from that time forward, they became Johnston's staunch friends. Liver-Eating Johnston outlived his fame and died at the Veterans Hospital in Los Angeles in 1900.

CRAZY WOMAN MORGAN AND THE MASSACRE

- 1846 -

No one knows what prompted John Morgan to pull his wagon from the emigrant train and strike out on his own across the endless prairie. Some say that Morgan and the wagon train master had a disagreement and that Morgan's Yankee independence convinced him he was better off finishing his trip to Oregon alone. Whatever the reason, Morgan, his wife, two small sons, and a teenaged daughter bid farewell to their friends somewhere in southeastern Nebraska, near the Oregon Trail's crossing of the Big Blue River.

For the next few weeks, the Morgans traveled alone, bound for a new life in Oregon. By the summer of 1846, they had gone about seven hundred miles and had to stop for several days to make repairs on their wagon. The region was so pleasant that Morgan decided to rest awhile there on the Musselshell River, a few miles south of its confluence with the Missouri. Morgan and his boys erected a lean-to, while his wife and daughter did the cooking and other domestic chores.

Each morning, Morgan released his weary oxen to graze on the sweetgrass that grew in the lowlands along the Musselshell. At night, for protection from wild animals, he brought the cattle back to the lean-to, tying them up until the next day.

The family had been at its temporary home for only three days when Morgan failed to return from retrieving the oxen for the evening. Mrs. Morgan sent the two boys to look for her husband, but they, too, didn't return. Still apparently unaware of any danger, Mrs. Morgan dispatched her daughter to search for the threesome and the missing oxen.

Shortly after the girl left the lean-to, her mother heard a distant scream. Grabbing an ax from the wagon, Mrs. Morgan ran in the direction of her daughter's shrieks. As she approached, she saw at least a dozen Indians, later identified as Blackfeet, in the midst of massacring her family.

John Morgan was tied to a large tree, and although he was still alive, his head dripped with blood as one brave jerked his scalp from his skull. Both boys were already dead, their heads smashed by repeated blows from the Indians' tomahawks. They, too, had been scalped. The Morgans' lovely daughter lay on the ground, barely breathing. Her clothes had been stripped from her body, and a Blackfeet brave crouched over her.

The warriors quickly regrouped and advanced toward Mrs. Morgan, expecting another easy victim. But, like a possessed woman, she lifted the ax above her head and started swinging it wildly. The braves were terrified as the crazy woman smashed the ax into the heads of first one and then another victim.

The Indians quickly killed the daughter and took her scalp. They cut Morgan from the tree, threw him across a horse, and then galloped away, dropping Morgan's scalp in their haste. They left behind four of their companions, victims of Mrs. Morgan's deadly ax.

Toward dusk John Johnston, still several months away from the personal tragedy that would haunt him for the rest of his life, rode onto the massacre scene while returning to a cabin he'd built on the Musselshell. Mrs. Morgan, still in a daze, wandered ax in hand from the body of one loved one to the next. Seeing the trapper, she raised her weapon and started toward him, but he quickly consoled her and convinced her that he was a friend.

Johnston spent the next few hours burying the remains of Mrs. Morgan's children on high ground near the lean-to. He dug an extra grave for her husband's scalp. Then he placed a sharpened post on top of each mound, and Mrs. Morgan stuck the heads of the four vanquished Blackfeet upon them.

During the next several days, Johnston built a small log cabin for Mrs. Morgan and stocked it with some of the supplies he was carrying to his own home. When he had finished the cabin to his liking, he decided it was time to leave. Later, he said that his departure was hastened when Mrs. Morgan "p'inted her musket at me. Pore critter, she had me skeart."

Like wildfire the story of "Crazy Woman" Morgan spread throughout the upper Missouri River basin. She refused to return to civilization and preferred to keep vigil over her four graves. She survived by foraging in the woods and accepting the benevolence of overland travelers and mountain men who had heard her story and who left food and other supplies near her cabin. Johnston stopped by whenever he was in the vicinity, but he could never get the woman to talk to him or leave the graves.

In time Mrs. Morgan died, a pitiful relic of the adventuresome woman who had arrived on the banks of the Musselshell years before. Neighboring Crow Indians, out of respect for this brave woman and out of their own hatred of the Blackfeet, carefully placed her emaciated body in a grave near her long-lost loved ones.

Some claim the Crazy Mountains of central Montana were named for the unfortunate woman.

FORT BENTON: MECCA ON THE UPPER MISSOURI

- 1860 -

STANDING AT THE HELM OF THE *Chippewa,* a 165-foot-long sternwheeler owned by Pierre Chouteau, Jr., and Company, Captain John LaBarge was excited this summer day in 1859. He and his ninety-five-man crew were taking the steamer from Fort Union at the mouth of the Yellowstone River to Fort Benton, some 650 miles up the Missouri.

Until now river traffic between the two forts had been restricted to flatboats because of the shallowness of the water in the extreme upper reaches of the Missouri. But the *Chippewa* drew only thirty-one inches, even with a full load. If LaBarge could make this trip successfully, he would open a new era of river transportation in the Far West.

As a crowd at Fort Benton eagerly awaited the approach of the steamer, a messenger rode up with news that the *Chippewa* had come within fifteen miles of its destination before running aground. Sadly, the throng dispersed, but Charles P. Chouteau, the organizer of the attempted journey, was anything but disheartened. He wrote to Secretary of War John B. Floyd:

> *By my present experience I have arrived at the conclusion that with suitable boats, and the removal of boulders here and there obstructing the channel and forming the rapids, that the navigation of the Upper Missouri can be made just as safe and easy as the Upper Mississippi and Ohio Rivers, and I have no hesitation in affirming that the trip from Saint Louis to Fort Benton can be easily accomplished within thirty-five days.*

Chouteau didn't have to wait long for his prophecy to come true. On July 2, 1860, the *Chippewa* and a companion vessel, the *Key West,* reached Fort Benton and launched a thriving river commerce that was to last until the advent in Montana of the railroad.

Fort Benton was built at a strategic location along the Missouri River, about thirty miles downstream from the Great Falls. Completed in 1846 by Alexander Culbertson and originally named Fort Lewis, the fort underwent changes in 1850 and was rechristened Fort Benton.

The fort was named after the original Fort Benton, which had been built in 1821 by the Missouri Fur Company at the mouth of the Bighorn River. The earlier fort, constructed primarily to accommodate fur trappers and traders among the Indians, was named in honor of Missouri's indomitable Senator Thomas Hart Benton, an advocate of westward expansion.

But the fur trade wasn't what gave the new Fort Benton its importance in the 1860s and 1870s. Rather, it was its critical location at the head of steamboat navigation. Numerous gold strikes in the region had brought prospectors by the thousands, and these emigrants and their families needed food, medical supplies, equipment, and building materials with which to construct some semblance of civilization on the Montana frontier. Also, a military road laid out by Lieutenant John Mullan had been completed in 1862, linking Fort Benton with Walla Walla in Washington Territory. This six-hundred-mile thoroughfare offered miners relatively easy access from Fort Benton to the rich goldfields in the newly created Idaho Territory, as well as those in western Montana.

William Conrad, an early Montana entrepreneur, once called Fort Benton a "business metropolis that had for its active business activities nearly a whole continent, that purchased goods from New Orleans on the south and the Great Slave Lake on the north, almost within the Arctic circle, and sold goods all over the world, in St. Louis and New York, in London and St. Petersburg, a business running into millions of dollars annually."

In 1867–1868, an estimated $24 million worth of gold was mined in Montana, and about 80 percent of it filtered through Fort Benton and down the Missouri to the eastern markets. But as the gold booms went bust, Fort Benton began to lose its prominence. By 1870 its population had fallen from 500 to 180, and only eight boats made the effort to put in at its wharves that year.

During its heyday Fort Benton served as a mecca to travelers in the vast Montana wilderness. It was a jumping-off place where miners could stock up on provisions before making the long trip into the depths of the Rocky Mountains. It was a shipping point that provided a commercial link between the goldfields of the frontier and St. Louis, some twenty-three hundred miles downriver.

When the railroad made water transportation in Montana obsolete, the small community of Fort Benton, which had grown up around the fort buildings, lost its bustle and languished on the prairie.

THE GOLDEN CORNERSTONE

- 1862 -

Gold has bewitched man since the beginning of civilization. It has caused empires to rise and fall, men to kill and be killed, and businesses to flourish and flounder.

In Montana, as in many western states, gold played a vital role in the settlement of the region. Indeed, as Michael P. Malone and Richard B. Roeder stated in their outstanding book, *Montana: A History of Two Centuries,* "Montana's foundation . . . stands upon a golden cornerstone."

No one knows exactly who discovered the first gold in Montana. It probably was an Indian who, one day in the distant past, noticed the sparkle of nuggets lying in a creek bed. But to the Native Americans who inhabited the region, gold had no intrinsic value, and they paid little attention to the mineral's profusion.

Many of the fur trappers who frequented the mountains and plains of Montana no doubt found specks of gold here and there. But like the Indians, the mountain men were creatures of the wilderness.

While they certainly understood the value of the metal, they had no time to settle down to prospecting. They were busy hunting riches of another kind.

In 1858 James and Granville Stuart made the first recorded discovery of gold in Montana—at Gold Creek, near present-day Drummond. The brothers, born in Virginia but raised in Iowa, had worked the California goldfields in the early 1850s. When the economy there began to sag, they wandered the West and came at last to Montana. The Stuarts' strike at Gold Creek did not prove very significant, and American Fork, the small settlement that sprang up there, was short lived.

Four years passed before Montana saw its first real gold rush. During the early 1860s miners from the overworked diggings of California and Colorado swarmed the region. One of them, John White, discovered a sizable placer deposit on Grasshopper Creek during the summer of 1862, and the rush was on. As hundreds of miners entered the area, Montana's first boomtown, Bannack City, was born.

Mining claims were issued out of the Bannack City land office as rapidly as they could be written. Before the end of 1862, the town's population had swollen to five hundred. While the region continued to grow and produce gold, a series of even larger finds eventually made Montana one of the most prolific gold producers in North America.

In 1863 James Stuart organized a prospecting party to explore the Yellowstone Valley. One of the group found gold while camped on the divide between the Jefferson and Madison Rivers, in a place he called Alder Gulch. Within eighteen months, more than ten thousand miners flooded the rocky region, and the boomtowns of Virginia City and Nevada City were founded. By the end of its first year, Virginia City claimed a population of ten thousand and was Montana's largest town. The placer mines around Alder Gulch produced close to $40 million worth of gold in their first five years.

Following the Alder Gulch discovery, a profusion of gold strikes occurred throughout Montana. In July 1864 another group of miners—known to history as the Four Georgians—discovered gold in Last Chance Gulch. Again, the stage was set for an unprecedented influx of prospectors into the area. The town of Helena was born, and it thrived amid the hectic activities that produced $19 million worth of gold in the first four years.

Confederate Gulch was the site of the next bonanza, which spawned Diamond City. This mining camp east of Helena in the Big Belt Mountains eventually housed ten thousand miners and their families and produced $30 million worth of gold.

Montana's gold rushes did far more than make a few people rich and a lot of people poor. The sudden influx of thousands of miners and their families created a need for food, hardware, machinery, and housing, as well as governmental representation. Those needs were satisfied in part by the creation of transportation and communications systems that allowed the free and fairly rapid exchange of ideas and the movement of commodities. In short, the most important result of the gold rushes was to propel Montana toward territorial status in 1864.

By 1866 Montana was the second largest gold-producing region in the country after California. The population of the territory rose to twenty-eight thousand, only to decline dramatically over the next few years as the luster of the gold rushes wore off. But by then the territory was becoming as civilized as the rest of the West, and its leaders were dreaming of statehood.

BLOOD ON THE BOZEMAN TRAIL

- 1863 -

In 1863 a twenty-nine-year-old Georgian named John Bozeman and his prospector partner John Jacobs decided to plot an easier, more convenient route from the Oregon Trail north to the Montana goldfields. Although aware that the Sioux and Cheyenne Indians favored the rich region along the Powder River east of the Bighorn Mountains, they blazed their trail through the heart of the Indians' hunting grounds.

Bozeman and Jacobs thought heavily armed wagon trains would be safe from Indian attacks along their trail, but the first train they led had to turn back because of menacing Sioux. Subsequent trains made it through, but continued attacks made travel extremely dangerous. People began clamoring for government protection along the route.

By 1865 the federal government was reeling under the immense financial strain of the Civil War. It needed to replenish its treasury—and soon. As news of the Montana gold strikes reached federal officials, they realized that they might have found an answer to their prayers. They saw the benefits of the Bozeman Trail, and so, in the spring of 1866, they ordered the construction of three forts along its route for the specific purpose of protecting Montana-bound immigrants.

The Bozeman Trail began in northeastern Colorado and ran through Nebraska and Wyoming to Virginia City, Montana. The three strategic forts were built along it during the summer of 1866 and garrisoned by the U.S. Army. Forts Reno and Phil Kearney were located in what is now Wyoming, while Fort C. F. Smith was situated in southern Montana.

A delegation of government officials met with the Indians and convinced them to sign a treaty permitting use of the Bozeman Trail. But the officials overlooked—or didn't understand—the fact that the treaty's signers didn't represent the hostile factions of the Sioux and Cheyenne tribes. Consequently, the construction of the three forts only aggravated an already strong enmity that was festering among the tribes' belligerent leaders.

In late December 1866 Captain William J. Fetterman and eighty men rode out of Fort Phil Kearney with orders to rescue a crew of woodcutters that had been attacked by Indians. Fetterman was told not to pursue the attackers, but he disregarded his instructions and rode into an ambush. Eighty-one men were slaughtered on that cold winter's day in a deadly conflict that signaled the beginning of the end for the Bozeman Trail.

The famous mountain man Jim Bridger, who was a civilian at Fort Phil Kearney at the time, wrote that

> *The only way to settle the question is to send out a sufficient number of troops to completely whip the hostile*

Sioux, Cheyennes and Arapahos and make them sue for peace. Unless this is done the [Bozeman] road had better be abandoned and the country given up to the Indians.

After the Fetterman Massacre the situation along the Bozeman Trail grew chaotic. The winter of 1866–1867 was intensely cold. All three forts were short of supplies, and their men almost froze to death.

In June the Indians renewed their attacks on Fort Phil Kearney and its woodcutting details. In early August there were fierce battles outside Forts C. F. Smith and Phil Kearney. It became obvious that there would be no peace in the region until the army evacuated.

Finally, on March 2, 1868, after untold suffering and loss of life, President Andrew Johnson ordered that Forts Phil Kearney, Reno, and C. F. Smith be abandoned. By midsummer the forts were empty, and the happy Indians burned all three to the ground.

THE INNOCENTS AT THE END OF THEIR ROPE

- 1864 -

TWENTY-SEVEN-YEAR-OLD HENRY PLUMMER was lying in bed when the idea occurred to him. He was restless and couldn't sleep because of a hacking cough, sneezing, and pain in his chest. He'd obviously caught a severe cold, probably from having been out in a storm.

As he lay there in his cell at San Quentin Prison on that July day in 1859, he began to formulate a scheme that might just get him out of jail. He would fake an illness and try to convince the prison authorities that he was dying. Maybe, if they believed him, they would release him and he would be free at last!

When doctors examined Plummer and saw the blood he'd supposedly coughed up onto his pillow, they said he had terminal consumption and probably only a few more weeks to live. Pleas from Plummer's friends outside the prison walls convinced officials to release him immediately and spare him the agony of dying behind bars. So, after serving not quite six months of a ten-year sentence for the second-degree murder of an unarmed man, Henry Plummer was free.

Plummer was born in Maine and gradually made his way west to Nevada City, California. Within a short time of his arrival, he was elected marshal. It was while serving in this role that he committed the crime that landed him in San Quentin.

After his release Plummer returned to Nevada City and was appointed assistant marshal. In 1861 after almost killing a man in a brawl, he left Nevada City and headed for Carson City, Nevada. Trouble in that town sent him back to Nevada City, where he stayed until he killed a man. He fled again to Carson City. Finally, Plummer and some of his associates went to Walla Walla, Washington, and then to Lewiston, Idaho.

While in Idaho, Plummer organized a bandit gang that made its living robbing miners and their camps. The members of the gang were all desperadoes who would kill at the drop of a hat. Although Plummer posed as a respectable gambler, he was the brains of the outfit and the one who kept it profitable. When a saloon keeper suspected Plummer's involvement in the numerous robberies that were occurring in the area, he was killed. Idaho vigilantes forced Plummer and his cohorts to move to Montana.

Gold was discovered in Montana in 1862, when Plummer and the remnants of his Idaho gang arrived at Deer Lodge. Realizing that he had an unprecedented opportunity to strike it rich, Plummer reorganized his band of outlaws and began a reign of terror throughout western Montana.

All the while, Plummer posed as a righteous pillar of the community. He was handsome and well dressed, and everyone believed him to be an intelligent, socially acceptable man about town. Eventually he was elected sheriff of Bannack and then of neighboring Virginia City as well. He even took a wife, Electa Bryan, the sister-in-law of the superintendent of the Blackfoot Indian school at Sun River.

Meanwhile, crime was rampant in Bannack and Virginia City. Scores of robberies and murders occurred with increasing frequency. And Plummer was the brain behind the well-orchestrated operation that kept townspeople and stagecoach operators on constant edge.

It was soon obvious that Sheriff Plummer was not going to restore peace and order. When the residents of Bannack and Virginia City could put up with the lawlessness no more, some of the leading citizens formed a Vigilance Committee. Their only recourse, they believed, was to take the law into their own hands.

The Vigilantes apprehended one of Plummer's gang, which went by the name "The Innocents," and forced him to reveal the names of the other members. A few of the Vigilantes had heard of Plummer's escapades elsewhere, but none had suspected that he was the ringleader of all the crimes from which they'd suffered lately. When they heard his name, their anger was almost uncontrollable. The sheriff they had elected was the primary source of all their troubles!

Plummer was asleep on a couch in the home of his wife's sister in Bannack when a loud knock on the door awakened him. His hostess escorted one of the Vigilantes into the living room where Plummer was lying. After a quiet discussion the two men left the house and were joined by several other Vigilantes in the yard. Together, they marched down the cold, snowy street to the gallows.

Plummer reportedly cried like a baby, begging his captors not to execute him. It was all to no avail. In the early morning hours of January 10, 1864, the smooth-talking outlaw sheriff was hanged from the very gallows that he had ordered built only a few days earlier.

JIM BECKWOURTH: ADOPTED SON OF THE CROWS

- 1866 -

In 1885 historian Hubert Howe Bancroft described Jim Beckwourth as "a famous hunter, guide, Indian-fighter, chief of the Crows, and horse-thief." Bancroft quickly added that "no resume can do justice to his adventures, nor can the slightest faith be put in his statements."

Bancroft referred to Beckwourth's biography, *The Life and Adventures of James P. Beckwourth, Mountaineer, Scout, and Pioneer, and Chief of the Crow Nation of Indians,* written by T. D. Bonner and published in New York in 1856. Bonner, a former newspaper journalist from New England, had run into Beckwourth in California during the gold rush. Fascinated by the yarns the old mountain man told, he had convinced Beckwourth to dictate his life's story for later publication.

Modern historians consider much of the boasting Beckwourth does in his biography to be so much fiction. But, on the other hand, they are quick to admit that most of the events he described really happened much as he said. All in all, the rare volume presents a picture of a happy-go-lucky man who loved the wilderness and who made an indelible mark on the West.

Beckwourth claims he was born in April 1798 in Fredericksburg, Virginia, one of thirteen children. His father was a Revolutionary War veteran whose own great-grandfather had been knighted by Charles II of England in 1681. Beckwourth's mother was a black slave.

As a boy Beckwourth moved with his family to the area around St. Charles, Missouri, where he worked as a blacksmith's apprentice, a hunter, and a lead miner. In the spring of 1825, the young man left St. Louis as a member of General William Ashley's trapping expedition to the Rocky Mountains. From that point on, Beckwourth knew his destiny lay with the beaver-trapping brotherhood of mountain men.

Beckwourth learned his new craft quickly and became a proficient trapper. After the 1825 season he returned to St. Louis, but he left again for the mountains the following spring, this time as a free trapper with Jedediah Smith.

During his time in the mountains, Beckwourth became familiar with most of the Indian tribes of the region. He was particularly fond of the Crows. By 1829 he had moved in with and been accepted by the tribe. He apparently married at least twice within the tribe and sired at least one son.

Beckwourth's restless spirit finally got the best of him, and he went off to California in 1835. He later served as a soldier in the Second Seminole War in Florida and was present at the Battle of Okeechobee in December 1837. His years between the Seminole expedition and the Civil War were filled with adventures in California and New Mexico.

In 1860 Beckwourth married again and settled down in Denver, where he ran a store and owned a small ranch south of town. In 1864 he guided the attack by Colonel J. M. Chivington's Third Colorado Volunteers on Black Kettle's Cheyenne encampment at Sand Creek. Later regretting his part in the unprovoked massacre of several hundred Indian women and children, he testified before a government committee, calling the atrocities that he had witnessed "revolting."

Beckwourth was a scout and messenger at Fort Laramie, in what is now Wyoming. Then Colonel Henry B. Carrington, the builder of Fort Phil Kearney, hired him to interpret among the Crows. His duties took him to Fort C. F. Smith on the Bighorn River. From there, he went to visit his old tribe and try to persuade them not to resist the army's presence along the Bozeman Trail.

Beckwourth took ill shortly after reaching the Crow villages. He died among his adopted people in 1866 and was buried on a scaffold, according to tribal custom. Before he died, he won the promise from the Crow leadership that they would support the army in its struggles with the Sioux and Cheyennes.

SHOOT-OUT IN THE HAY FIELDS

- 1867 -

On a morning in July 1867, scouts of the Sioux chief Red Cloud watched several wagons bearing wooden crates rumble through the gates of Fort C. F. Smith. Had they known what those crates contained, they might have been less anxious to attack a party of men mowing hay outside the fort nine days later.

As it turned out, the boxes were filled with new Springfield breech-loading, .50-caliber rifles. Although capable of firing only a single shot at a time, the guns were vastly superior to muzzle-loading arms, and they gave a decided advantage to anyone who owned them. Soon after the rifles arrived, they were distributed to the men at the fort.

Fort Smith wasn't a large post. It measured about 125 yards square and was dominated by a watchtower at the southeast corner. Cannons were mounted at opposite corners of the stockade so that they could defend all four walls. Because of the placement of the fort and the lay of the land around it, the army believed nothing could move within a mile in any direction during the day without being observed.

With summer, the men at the fort needed to cut the hay that would feed the many mules and horses confined there during the winter. The most luxurious hay fields were about two and a half miles from the fort, and marauding Indians made the job of mowing them extremely dangerous. Two soldiers had been killed the previous year while attempting the task.

In late June a party of civilians got ready for the mowing by building a corral in the hay-fields to protect their animals at night and serve as a fortification for the men in case of attack. They erected tents in which to sleep and cook.

The hay-cutting party consisted of twenty-five men—nineteen soldiers armed with the new Springfield rifles and six civilians, some of whom carried repeating Spencer and Henry rifles. All in all, it was a pretty-well-armed contingent that set out to gather the hay as rapidly as possible.

On July 31 a party of Crow Indians rode by the hay fields and told the men that they were about to be attacked by a large group of Sioux warriors. The men dismissed the tale as fiction, and the Crows moved on to the fort itself, repeating the warning there. Soldiers at the fort didn't believe the Crows either. They thought the Indians were merely trying to scare them.

They changed their minds the following morning when the haycutters were attacked in the fields. Making their way safely to the protective corral, the mowing party realized that several hundred Indians were bearing down on them from the valley to the northeast.

Second Lieutenant Sigmund Sternberg was in command of the hay-cutting detail. He was killed almost immediately, leaving a civilian, D. A. Colvin, to take charge. Colvin had served as a Union captain during the Civil War and was quickly able to take control.

Armed with a Henry repeating rifle and a thousand rounds of ammunition, he personally killed or wounded 150 warriors, according to later reports.

The Indians were outgunned, but the hay cutters were severely outnumbered. In the end the guns prevailed. The battle dragged on for most of the day, as the Sioux warriors made repeated attempts to destroy the small contingent of soldiers and civilians. They ignited the hay with flaming arrows, they killed or disabled most of the mules, and they shot at the crew from distant vantage points.

When most of the Indians finally retreated, a messenger raced to the fort. The commander, Lieutenant Colonel L. P. Bradley, had been aware of the struggle in the hay fields but had chosen not to send a relief column for fear the Indians would attack and overrun the weakened garrison. When the messenger rode through the gates, Bradley dispatched two companies to the hay fields.

The number of casualties from the battle in the hay field was never accurately determined. But fort records indicated that eight Indians were killed and thirty more wounded. Two soldiers and one civilian apparently were killed, and three soldiers were wounded.

If the soldiers hadn't been armed with the new Springfield rifles with their improved breech-loading mechanism, the hay-field battle might have been a victory for the Sioux. As it turned out, the superior weapons of the army, coupled with the repeating Henrys and Spencers of the civilians, saved the day.

POINTING THEM NORTH ON THE TEXAS TRAIL

- 1870 -

WHEN BOTH CONFEDERATE AND UNION SOLDIERS RETURNED home to Texas after the Civil War, they found a land far different from the one they'd left behind. In 1860 assessors had counted some three and a half million head of cattle in the state. But left in the care of old men, boys, and slaves, the livestock multiplied. By the war's end at least five million cattle—probably many more—roamed the grasslands and brush country of the Lone Star State.

The returning soldiers found their farms and ranches ruined by lack of supervision. The vast herds of longhorn cattle ran wild and unattended, and the state's finances were in a shambles. Yet those very cattle held the solution to the problem. Wise men saw that the animals could ease the hunger pangs of the growing cities back East and in the Mississippi River valley. The only problem was getting the herds to market.

A few herds had already trailed north from Texas before the Civil War, but it was the period of depression after the conflict that opened the door to the great Texas cattle drives. Joseph G. McCoy had the idea first. Since the railroad had reached Abilene, Kansas, in 1867, why not drive the Texas cattle the few hundred miles north to the railhead, where they could be packed into railroad cars and economically shipped east?

McCoy found Abilene to be a small village of only twelve or so log cabins, most of which had dirt roofs. He speedily set his plan in motion and built stockyards, offices, a hotel, and holding pens near the railroad in anticipation of the thousands of cattle that would soon be trekking through downtown Abilene. It was the beginning of an era, and one that would make the Texas cowboy an enduring American hero.

Some thirty-five thousand cattle arrived at Abilene during the summer of 1867. A train pulling twenty cars full of Texas longhorns left town in September headed for the stockyards at Chicago. Not much money was made on this initial experiment, but the knowledge that long-range transportation could be realistically accomplished helped determine the fate of the nation and the fortunes of hundreds of future cattlemen.

As the railroad progressed westward, the cattle trails that accommodated the railhead towns shifted as well. In time, as the popularity of the Northwest grew, Texas cattle were driven to Montana to take advantage of the rich grazing lands there. Before long the entire region was full of cowboys who had worked their way up the Texas Trail.

"The Texas Trail was no mere cow-path," wrote one historian in 1892. "It was the course of empire." And a cattle empire was exactly what the trail promoted during the 1870s and 1880s. With its beginnings in South Texas, the trail headed northward, passing through

Fort Worth, Texas; Camp Supply, Oklahoma; Dodge City, Kansas; and Ogallala and Fort Robertson, Nebraska. It crossed parts of South Dakota and Wyoming before ending in central Montana. Before the great cattle drives were over, replaced by more modern modes of transportation, millions of Texas longhorns had made the long trek, watched over by countless thousands of nameless cowboys.

One of the most famous of these cowboys was a slight, thin-faced Englishman by the name of E. C. "Teddy Blue" Abbott. Abbott's father had settled in Nebraska when his son was eleven years old, so the lad literally grew up beside the Texas Trail. Montana laid claim to him in 1883 when he drove his first cattle out of Texas and into what was then Montana Territory.

Life on the trail was full of trials and tribulations. In the book *Back-Trailing on the Old Frontiers,* Teddy Blue described events as they occurred on the rigorous northward journey:

> *The boys would start north with from 1,500 to 2,000 cattle that were wild as buffaloes and take them a thousand miles through an unknown country. . . . When a stampede started, the cowboys guarding the herd would pull their six-shooters and begin shooting as they swung the lead and tried to throw the fear-crazed cattle into a mill, which means to get them running in a circle instead of streaking off over the prairie. . . . Every cowpuncher realized the peril of trying to head a stampede, but I can say with truth that I never knew one to falter or shirk. . . . Loss of sleep was the worst thing on the trail. I've many a time rubbed tobacco in my eyes to keep them open. . . . A day's drive was some-*

> *times as long as 40 miles, but the average was only 10 to 15 miles, according to water. . . . The boys always took great pride in getting the herd through in good shape. . . . They were surely loyal to their employers and to one another.*

Because of accounts like those of Teddy Blue, the romance and excitement of the cowboys and their cattle drives continue to live on in the nation's imagination.

KING COPPER

- 1876 -

By the mid-1860s the word "gold" was on the lips of everyone in Montana. Rich strikes in the early sixties had attracted prospectors and miners by the thousands, and they were interested in no other mineral, except perhaps the silver that was often found in association with gold.

As early as 1856, when a group of travelers passed the site of the future city of Butte, one of the men in the party, Caleb Irvine, discovered strands of copper ore in some rough rock outcrops. But after ensuring that there was no gold or silver, Irvine left the region, unaware that he had just stumbled upon what was to become the largest copper mine in the world.

It took another man, a poor immigrant miner from Ireland named Marcus Daly, to realize the importance of the copper in and around Butte. Daly, who had come to America at the age of fifteen, had worked in the gold camps in California, Nevada, and Utah before heading to Montana in 1876.

The Walker brothers of Salt Lake City had purchased some diggings near Butte called the Alice Mine. They sent Daly to supervise the project and in return for his services gave him 25 percent ownership in the mine. Although the ambitious Daly was keenly interested in the mine's gold and silver prospects, he also was quick to recognize its copper-mining potential. He couldn't interest the Walker brothers in exploiting the copper, so he sold his shares in the Alice Mine and purchased the nearby Anaconda Mine, a silver mine that was also rich in copper.

Just about that time, an event occurred back East that would drastically change Daly's life and the economic life of Montana. On March 7, 1876, Alexander Graham Bell was awarded a patent for the telephone, a magical device that could transmit human voices across hundreds of miles. And, providential for Daly, the medium of transmission was copper wire.

For the next few years, in part because of the popularity of the telephone and the newly developed electricity—which also used copper wire—Daly's fortune grew. His mines provided work for hundreds and then thousands of laborers. Montana soon became such a focus of labor union activity that it was called the "Gibraltar of Unionism."

Daly was a shrewd businessman. He quickly saw the need for other industries in the region. His mines needed timber for shoring up the shafts, so Daly became involved in the lumber business. Some economical means was needed to transport the tons of copper ore brought to the surface each day, so he built his own railroad. And, in order to refine the ore into usable metal, he built his own smelter at nearby Anaconda, one of the classic company towns of the West.

By 1885 Butte had become the greatest mining camp in the West, and Daly and his Anaconda Company were a force to be reckoned with. Daly was respected by most of his peers and liked by many of his laborers. But like most men who wield vast power, he made enemies, too. One of the most powerful was William A. Clark.

A well-educated Pennsylvanian from an affluent family, Clark had built the first copper and silver smelter and the first waterworks in the Butte area. He soon amassed his own fortune in copper. For a time Daly and Clark cooperated in their common financial interest, but politics soon drove them apart. When Clark ran for Congress in 1888, Daly—who had political reasons for opposing him—used his influence to engineer Clark's humiliating defeat. This was only the first in a series of political losses that Clark would suffer at the hands of the Daly forces. In 1894 the two men even battled over the location of the state capital—Anaconda, controlled by Daly, or Helena, championed by Clark. This time, Clark won out.

Another "copper king," Frederick Augustus Heinze was the son of a wealthy German immigrant family. He received a degree in mining engineering in 1889 and came to Butte the same year. By 1899–1900, the swashbuckling Heinze had become the most controversial man in Montana mining. He maintained that whoever owned the property on which a vein of copper touched the surface also owned the entire vein, even though it might stretch for miles beneath someone else's property. This belief threw Heinze into pitched battle with Amalgamated Copper Company, the giant foreign trust to which Daly had sold his mining interests. After a series of bitter court battles, bribes, and a complete shutdown of Amalgamated enterprises, the trust beat Heinze—and Montana—into submission.

After Heinze's defeat Amalgamated consolidated its grip on Montana mining. In 1910 it bought Clark's copper mines and smelter and merged all its subsidiaries into the Anaconda Copper Mining Company. For almost half a century, Anaconda dominated the politics and economy of Montana.

Copper production is still big business in Montana, and the green ore is very much a part of the state's history and heritage. But the copper era provided more than mere metal for America's growing industries. It also was responsible for the eight-hour workday and an equitable pay scale for miners nationwide. For everyone associated with it—directly and indirectly—copper was "king" in Montana for many years.

A SIOUX CHIEF'S ACCOUNT OF CUSTER'S LAST STAND

- 1876 -

For more than a century, Americans have heard accounts of the battle along the Little Bighorn River in which Lieutenant Colonel George Armstrong Custer and his entire command were wiped out by Sioux and Cheyenne warriors. Most of these accounts have been written from the white man's viewpoint and are based on circumstantial evidence, since there were no army survivors to explain what happened. Few people bothered to interview the victorious Indians to get their side of the story.

But there is an obscure, eyewitness account of the Battle of the Little Bighorn, which took place in southern Montana in 1876. Its author is Flying Hawk, a Sioux chief who participated in the fight when he was twenty-four years old. Flying Hawk belonged to the Oglala clan. One of his brothers was Kicking Bear, who introduced the Ghost Dance to the Sioux. Sitting Bull was an uncle by marriage, and Crazy Horse was Flying Hawk's cousin and best friend.

Flying Hawk dictated his version of Custer's defeat to a white man, M. I. McCreight, probably during the late 1920s. McCreight had visited the Sioux much earlier, during the tribe's last glorious days of freedom, and for years afterwards Sioux friends were frequent guests at his home in Pennsylvania.

According to Flying Hawk, the battle began just before the Indians' dinner meal, when mounted soldiers charged the Sioux encampment and began firing into the tipis, hitting several women and children. He described the attack by Major Marcus Reno's command like this:

> *The Indian men got their horses and guns as quick as they could and went after the soldiers. Kicking Bear and Crazy Horse were in the lead. There was thick timber and when they got out of the timber there was where the first of the fight was.*

Flying Hawk told how his companions killed many soldiers with bows and arrows and noted that Crazy Horse personally quieted a great number with his war club. The river's steep banks impeded the soldiers' escape, and many men were slaughtered before they could scramble out of the water. The Indians continued their fight up the slope to the spot that Custer had picked to defend.

> *When Custer got nearly to the lower end of the camp, he started to go down a gulch, but the Indians were surrounding him, and he tried to fight. They got off their horses and made a stand but it was no use. Their horses ran down the ravine right into the village. The*

> *squaws caught them as fast as they came. . . . When we got them surrounded the fight was over in one hour. There was so much dust we could not see much, but the Indians rode around and yelled the war-whoop and shot into the soldiers as fast as they could until they were all dead. . . . We got off our horses and went and took the rings and money and watches from the soldiers. We took some clothes off too, and all the guns and pistols. We got seven hundred guns and pistols. Then we went back to the women and children and got them together that were not killed or hurt. It was hard to hear the women singing the death-song for the men killed and for the wailing because their children were shot while they played in the camp. It was a big fight; the soldiers got just what they deserved this time. No good soldiers would shoot into the Indian's teepee where there were women and children. These soldiers did, and we fought for our women and children. White men would do the same if they were men.*

Flying Hawk said the Sioux didn't mutilate the bodies of the soldiers as whites contended but merely took what possessions they wanted and could use. He said the Indians could have killed more of the soldiers who weren't fighting directly under Custer, but "they were glad to let us alone, and so we let them alone, too."

The Indians struck camp and left the area the following day. According to Flying Hawk, there were about twelve hundred Sioux and Cheyenne warriors at the Little Bighorn, but probably no more than one thousand participated in the battle, since some of the men were away hunting at the time. Among the well-known warriors who took part in the fight were Rain-in-the-Face, Sitting Bull, Lame Deer, Spotted Eagle, Crazy Horse, and Kicking Bear. The Cheyennes were led by Two Moon.

Flying Hawk visited his friend McCreight for the last time in 1929, when the old warrior was seventy-seven years old and in failing health. He died at the Pine Ridge Agency on Christmas Eve 1931, one of the last survivors of the Battle of the Little Bighorn.

"I WILL FIGHT NO MORE FOREVER"

- 1877 -

THE MORNING OF OCTOBER 1, 1877, was a memorable one for Captain Henry Romeyn. Under the command of Colonel Nelson Miles, he joined battle that day with Chief Joseph and his Nez Perce people, who had been trying to escape to Canada. The infantry commander would later describe that day of battle in the Bears Paw Mountains of north-central Montana like this:

> *Some of the soldiers had died during the night and many of the wounded were suffering terribly. Fifty or more wounded lay huddled together in a little hollow place. A storm set in and four or five inches of snow fell, adding to the torture of the stricken.*

Chief Joseph and his small band of men, women, and children had begun their flight earlier in the year, when the tribe was ordered by the federal government to vacate its extensive homeland in Idaho and settle on a much smaller reservation along the Clearwater River. The Nez Perce tried to resist peacefully but to no avail, and they finally and sorrowfully agreed to do as they were told. But in June, as they prepared to move, some bitter young warriors killed a few white settlers. The army mounted an attack.

After a couple of battles with U.S. soldiers in Idaho, the Indians crossed into Montana, hoping eventually to reach Canada and seek assistance from the Sioux chief Sitting Bull, who had already found refuge there. On August 9 an army force under Colonel John Gibbon clashed with Joseph's entourage in the Big Hole Valley in southwestern Montana. Although eighty-nine Indians were killed, the Nez Perce fought fiercely, broke away, and continued their march to destiny.

The Nez Perce entered the newly created Yellowstone National Park, where they terrorized several tourists. Although soldiers attempted to close all exits from the park, Joseph's hardy little band escaped and headed north.

When Joseph and his followers reached the Bears Paw Mountains on September 29, they were tired and cold. Although they were only forty miles from the international border and safety, they decided to stop to rest for the night. They would continue their march the next day.

Meanwhile, Colonel Miles had left Fort Keogh with nearly four hundred soldiers and a company of Sioux and Cheyenne scouts, as well as a couple of pieces of artillery. At eight o'clock on the morning of September 30, the soldiers attacked the surprised Nez Perce camp along Snake Creek.

The fighting was fierce. Miles attacked three times and was repelled. In the first charge about sixty officers and enlisted men were killed or wounded. Even the artillery seemed useless against the Nez Perce.

The fighting dragged on throughout the day. Romeyn recalled that

> *As the sun sank a white flag was raised and Joseph appeared. His clothes were pierced with a dozen bullets but he was uninjured. He proposed that he be permitted to march toward Canada, his warriors armed and mounted, but the proposal was rejected. The siege continued until the third of October, when Joseph and Miles again met in council and Joseph's proposal of a truce for his warriors with all the honors of war, they to retain their arms and property, was again rejected. On the morning of the fourth the gun was moved and the second shell fired from it killed and wounded a dozen Nez Perces. For the third time Joseph raised the white flag and this time it meant surrender.*

So ended the Nez Perce War of 1877. After a journey of fifteen hundred miles and the death of scores of their companions, the cold, hungry Indians surrendered to Colonel Miles. Chief Joseph is said to have proclaimed:

> *I am tired of fighting. Our chiefs are killed. Looking Glass is dead. . . . The old men are all dead. . . . It is cold, and we have no blankets. The little children are freezing to death. I want to have time to look for my children, and see how many of them I can find. Maybe I shall find them among the dead. Hear me, my chiefs! I am tired. My heart is sick and sad. From where the sun now stands I will fight no more forever.*

THE SLAUGHTER OF THE BUFFALO

- 1883 -

Of the many species of wildlife that greeted early explorers of the West, the bison made one of the most profound impressions. Even the earliest American settlers were familiar with the animal—commonly known as the buffalo—because its original range extended almost all the way to the Atlantic Ocean. But it wasn't until settlers moved onto the Great Plains that they realized just how prolific the big beast was. Seemingly endless herds blackened the prairie, providing the Indians with everything from food and clothing to shelter and utensils.

Yet, in a surprisingly short time, the buffalo would come perilously close to vanishing from the face of the earth. By the 1830s none could be found east of the Mississippi River, and Josiah Gregg, an early traveler on the Santa Fe Trail, commented that buffalo were "rarely seen within two hundred miles of the frontier."

As early as 1855 the U.S. government tried to protect the buffalo, but it failed miserably. By then the magnificent beast had become a target for every hide hunter, sportsman, and target shooter west of the Mississippi. One of these, an English nobleman named Sir George Gore, killed 2,000 buffalo, 1,600 deer and elk, and 105 bears during a single outing along the Platte and Missouri Rivers in the mid-1850s.

The mass slaughter continued after the Civil War. As Indian tribes unwillingly abandoned their homelands to increasing numbers of farmers, cattlemen, and miners, the buffalo's numbers dwindled. First, the hide hunters, or buffalo runners, decimated the herds roaming the southern plains, taking the hides and leaving the meat to rot in the sun. Then they focused their attention on the northern range.

But hunters feeding a national fancy for buffalo robes were not the only reason for the rapid obliteration of the species. As the army battled to subdue the Indians of the West, the government realized that the extermination of the buffalo could mean an end to the tribes that depended on the beast for their daily subsistence. Officials changed their minds about protecting the animal and instead began to encourage its annihilation.

General Philip Sheridan, commander of the army's Division of the Missouri, was reported to have said in 1875 that

> *The buffalo hunters have done in the last two years and will do more in the next year to settle the vexed Indian question, than the entire regular army has done in the last thirty years. They are destroying the Indian's commissary, and it is a well-known fact that an army losing its base of supplies is placed at a great disadvantage. Send them powder and lead, if you will; for the sake of a lasting peace, let them kill, skin and sell until the buffaloes are exterminated.*

Given this mentality among high government officials, the fate of the American bison was sealed.

When the southern herds were nearly gone, the hide hunters began operating out of Miles City, Montana. Phenomenal herds still grazed on the northern plains. U.S. Marshal X. Biedler of Montana told of traveling in 1879 through a herd that extended for seventy miles!

But the buffalo of the northern plains were doomed to the same fate as their fellows in Texas, Kansas, and Nebraska. By 1883 the Montana and Dakota herds had almost disappeared, and most of the hide hunters had either found new occupations or migrated to Canada to continue their gruesome work there.

In early 1886 William Hornaday, the chief taxidermist at the U.S. National Museum in Washington, D.C., went west to look for buffalo specimens for a new exhibit at the Smithsonian Institution. He had heard alarming reports that the bison was extinct, and he decided he could wait no longer. Arriving at Miles City, Hornaday's party started its search immediately. After eight weeks of frantic hunting, the group finally found twenty-five specimens, which were killed and mounted for display. The following year, a party from the American Museum of Natural History traveled to the same area and in three months saw not a single buffalo.

The nation's original buffalo population is officially estimated to have been sixty million animals. Today, after careful management, some three hundred and fifty thousand remain, most of them scattered on preserves such as the National Bison Range south of Montana's Flathead Lake.

THE HARD WINTER

- 1886-1887 -

In Montana Mother Nature is never so cruel as in winter, when temperatures can plunge well below zero and snow can reach the rooftops. And no Montana winter in recent history was more cruel than the "Hard Winter of 1886–1887." Never before or since have white inhabitants experienced such extremely cold temperatures for such a long time. As a direct result of that devastating winter, ranchers learned that they couldn't depend on the open range to support their livestock year-round, and they began to provide shelter and food in winter months.

The spring and summer of 1886 were exceptionally hot and dry. As early as May and June, sweltering temperatures were being recorded, and rainfall became so rare that many streams and watering holes dried up. Prairie fires were rampant, burning thousands of acres of the parched grassland. Some sections of the territory had received less than two inches of rain in twelve months.

As the cooler days of fall approached, the open range in Montana supported more cattle than ever before—possibly more than one million animals. What little grass had survived the drought was heavily overgrazed. There were indications that the winter would be severe. Granville Stuart, the owner of the DHS Ranch, one of the largest in Montana, recalled that many birds that usually wintered on the range disappeared, and the cattle grew unusually thick coats of hair. "Teddy Blue" Abbott, who worked as a cowboy for Stuart at the time, remembered seeing his first arctic owls, which usually lived farther north.

Two weeks of fair weather just before Christmas made the ranchers hopeful, but on Christmas Eve the snow began to fall. By December 27 the Missouri River at Fort Benton had frozen solid, and the weather station at Fort Assiniboine registered a temperature of thirty-seven degrees below zero. Temperatures across the territory hung below zero for days on end. Teddy Blue wrote years later that the Christmas Eve storm lasted sixty continuous days.

On February 3, 1887, the temperature at Fort Assiniboine dropped to 55.4 degrees below zero—the lowest ever recorded there. With the windchill factor it was ninety-five degrees below zero. Cattle began dying like flies. What little grass remained was frozen beneath several feet of snow, and the hungry livestock cut their feet and legs trying to paw through the icy crust to get at it. As author Joseph Kinsey Howard described it:

> *Starving cattle staggered through village streets, collapsed and died in dooryards. Five thousand head invaded the outskirts of the newborn city of Great Falls, bawling for food. They snatched up the saplings the proud city had just planted, gorged themselves upon garbage.*

Cattle weren't the only ones suffering from the severe cold. The residents of the small towns of Montana were faced with shortages of supplies, especially coal, flour, and wood. By the time the storm ended in March, there was almost no fuel left at Fort Benton. What few supplies were still available commanded exorbitant prices: coal, $60 a ton; flour, $7 a sack; and green wood, $20 a cord. Potatoes weren't available at any price.

A person had to be insane to go out in such weather, but the cowboys believed they had no choice. They worked day and night, for weeks on end, trying to rescue what cattle they could from freezing and starvation. Teddy Blue, in his book *We Pointed Them North,* described what he wore on the range: two pairs of wool socks, a pair of moccasins, a pair of Dutch socks that came to the knees, a pair of overshoes, two suits of heavy underwear, pants, overalls, chaps, a heavy shirt, wool gloves, heavy mittens, a blanket-lined sourdough overcoat, and a sealskin cap. Even with all these clothes, he noted, he didn't stay very warm.

Throughout February the storm raged. Finally, in March, warm chinook winds moderated temperatures. The snow vanished quickly, and thermometers at Fort Assiniboine read forty-six degrees above zero. The ice that had clogged the Missouri River melted, causing floods downstream.

Teddy Blue reported that, of the forty thousand cattle grazing the DHS Ranch in the fall of 1886, including ten thousand newly branded calves, fewer than seven thousand head, including only about one hundred yearlings, were counted the following spring. He estimated that 60 percent of all the cattle in Montana had perished during the winter. Their bloated bodies lay scattered across the countryside.

Many of the large ranches failed as a result of the disastrous winter. Some had been heavily in debt to begin with. The survivors made sure they never put their valuable stock in such a vulnerable position again. The days of the open range were numbered.

"LADY" CAMERON: MONTANA PHOTOGRAPHER

- 1889 -

PHOTOGRAPHY WAS PROBABLY THE LAST THING ON Evelyn Cameron's mind when she and her husband, Ewen, left England in 1889. The newlyweds were headed for Eastern Montana, a remote and desolate country that was already home to a small number of upper-class Britons who were raising ponies on the open range. It was a time of new beginnings, and Evelyn and Ewen were anxious to make their own mark on America's newest state.

The couple settled near Terry, a tiny village that had only a saloon, an engine tank, and a store, according to Evelyn. Curious neighbors called her "Lady" Cameron, no doubt because of her crisp British accent and regal bearing.

The Camerons were both from upper-class British families, and consequently they liked well-bred horses. They hoped to make their fortune from the rich grasslands of eastern Montana by raising polo ponies for export back to England. The venture ended in disaster when many of their ponies died of pneumonia while crossing the Atlantic. Those that survived were considered too wild for polo. The Camerons were financially devastated.

During the lean times that followed, Evelyn may have pondered her reasons for coming to America. She had been financially comfortable in England. Her half brother was Lord Battersea, a member of Prime Minister Gladstone's cabinet, and she, herself, had been socially prominent. But that was not enough for Evelyn and Ewen, a Scottish naturalist. They had read and heard so much about the great American West that they simply had to see it for themselves.

After the pony debacle Ewen devoted himself mostly to studying Montana birds. Evelyn threw herself into managing their frontier household. In 1894, perhaps influenced by a wealthy Irish boarder, Evelyn had ordered a camera through the mail and had become interested in photography. During the next several years, with no formal training, she became highly skilled at the art. It became her second love after her husband. And it became a way of supplementing their meager income.

Evelyn photographed everything and anything. She took pictures of wildlife to illustrate articles her husband had published in *The Auk,* the official journal of the American Ornithologists' Union. She was equally at ease photographing the daily activities of local residents, including cowboys, sheepherders, trappers, homesteaders, and railroad workers. She also chronicled her own life on the rugged frontier.

Ewen Cameron died of cancer in 1915, leaving Evelyn to run their small ranch alone. Her household chores never detracted from her zest for photography. For the next thirteen years, until her own death in 1928, she continued to be a common sight in and around Terry, although her outstanding contribution wasn't truly appreciated in her own lifetime.

Evelyn had willed all of her belongings to a close friend and neighbor, Janet Williams. These included her photography equipment and supplies, photographic plates and prints, and personal diaries, which sat in Williams's basement until 1979. Then a writer researching frontier women discovered them and included some of them in a book, *Photographing Montana 1894–1928: The World of Evelyn Cameron.*

The book by Donna M. Lucey presents 170 of Evelyn's finest photographs, less than 10 percent of the total discovered at the Williams home. It also contains poignant musings from Evelyn's diaries. Together, the words and images reveal a sensitive woman who transcended the hardships of her adopted home to become an accomplished chronicler of life on the Montana frontier.

THE BIRTH OF GLACIER NATIONAL PARK

- 1910 -

In the spring of 1876, George Bird Grinnell was sorely disappointed. Lieutenant Colonel George Armstrong Custer had personally invited him to accompany the Seventh Cavalry on a foray into Sioux country. Ordinarily young Grinnell would have been happy to accept. He knew Custer well and had ridden with him during the 1874 Black Hills Expedition. But this time Grinnell had too much work to do back at Yale University. He respectfully declined the invitation.

Of course, Custer and his command were massacred by Sioux and Cheyenne Indians in June 1876 during the Battle of the Little Bighorn. If Grinnell had gone along, he, too, probably would have been killed, and Glacier National Park might never have been born.

A native of Brooklyn, Grinnell was an outspoken outdoorsman and a professional naturalist. He became the natural history editor of *Forest and Stream* magazine in 1876 and was awarded a doctorate degree by Yale in 1880. He used his magazine to promote the primitive beauty and variety of the Glacier region and made several trips there himself in the late 1880s.

In 1886 Grinnell founded the Audubon Society and became editor of *Audubon* magazine. The following year, he and Theodore Roosevelt organized the Boone and Crockett Club, and in later years he served as its longtime president. Both groups still exist today, tributes to the organizational skills of this champion for the conservation of America's natural resources.

By 1883 the idea of preserving the beautiful Glacier region for future generations had been proposed. That year, a young army lieutenant, John Van Orsdale, wrote to a local newspaper:

> *I sincerely hope that publicity now being given to that portion of Montana will result in drawing attention to the scenery which surpasses anything in Montana or adjacent territories. A great benefit would result to Montana if this section could be set aside as a National Park. The country included in such a park is not fit for agricultural or grazing purposes but by placing it under the protection of the Government the forests would be protected and consequently some of the sources of water of three great river systems, viz: the Missouri, the Columbia, and the Saskatchewan.*

In 1891, when the Great Northern Railway pushed through the Glacier area, Grinnell first argued that the surrounding forests, streams, and mountains should be protected by the government. The precedent was there. Yellowstone had been designated a national park in 1872 and Yosemite in 1890.

In an article for *Century* magazine, Grinnell wrote:

> *No words can describe the grandeur and majesty of these mountains, and even photographs seem hopelessly to dwarf and belittle the most impressive peaks. The fact that it is altogether unknown, the beauty of its scenery, its varied and unusual fauna, and the opportunity it offers for hunting and fishing and for mountain climbing, give the region a wonderful attraction for the lover of nature.*

The management of the Great Northern Railway also deserves credit for helping to make Glacier a national park. As the railroad cut through the northern Montana wilderness, its officials were quick to realize the potential for tourism in this remote part of America. As Grinnell later said, "Important men in control of Great Northern Railroad were made to see the possibilities of the region and after nearly twenty years of effort, a bill setting aside the park was passed."

The legislation was signed into law May 11, 1910, by President William Howard Taft. An excited Montana congressman, Charles N. Pray, scribbled a note to Grinnell that day, advising him that

> *I have just been notified by telephone from the White House that the President had just signed the Glacier National Park bill. The bill has now become a law and I sincerely hope that someday in the near future, when you are in the West on your summer vacation, that I may have the great pleasure of meeting you in the new National Park. With many thanks for your*

> *assistance in creating a sentiment favorable to this measure. . . .*

With the creation of Glacier National Park, Grinnell's name became forever linked with that of Montana. Although he never permanently lived in the state, Grinnell loved and appreciated the Montana wilderness. His leadership in preserving the beauty of Glacier makes him a Montanan in spirit.

SHELBY'S DAY OF GLORY

- 1923 -

"Champion Wins" read the headline in the *Shelby Promotor's* special "Fight Edition" of July 4, 1923. Almost the entire front page was devoted to news of the boxing event that had ended only a few hours before the newspaper hit the streets of the small town in northcentral Montana.

Under a secondary headline that said "20,000 People Watch Thrilling Title Bout," the story of the now-famous Jack Dempsey–Tommy Gibbons heavyweight duel continued:

> *Under a broiling sun, uncomfortable in some degree to the fans, but ideal from the standpoint of the fighting man, Jack Dempsey this afternoon successfully defended his title as heavyweight champion of the world. Although Dempsey won, the champ knows he has been through the hardest fight of his ring career, and the loser came off with almost as much glory as the winner.*

The fight—which generated international interest—began as a mere publicity gimmick. James W. "Body" Johnson, the son of the first mayor of Shelby, was looking for a way to promote his ailing real estate business, give the local economy a boost, and focus outside attention on his remote section of Montana. He decided to arrange a fight between Dempsey, the reigning world heavyweight boxing champion, and Tommy Gibbons, an impressive fighter with more than eighty-eight bouts under his belt and only one loss.

Johnson hatched his idea after reading in the local paper that someone in Montreal had offered Dempsey's manager $100,000 to bring the champ to Canada. Not to be outdone—but with absolutely no intention of really consummating the deal—he sent off a wire to Jack Kearns, Dempsey's manager, offering $200,000 if Dempsey would come to Shelby to fight Gibbons.

Johnson was amazed when several days later Kearns accepted the invitation.

Undaunted and aware that his scheme had gone too far to back out, Johnson sought and received the support of Montana's governor, Joe Dixon, and the state chairman of the American Legion, Loy J. Molumby. The national office of the Legion issued a statement insisting it had nothing to do with the deal. The organization considered Dempsey a shirker because he had performed civilian work in the United States during World War I instead of joining the military with other young men his age.

When Johnson realized that the fight was actually going to occur, he quickly began raising the money needed to stage it. An octagonal stadium capable of seating more than forty thousand people was erected on twenty acres of land within Shelby's city limits at a cost of $82,000. Tickets were printed, with ringside seats selling for $50. The Great Northern Railway threw up temporary train depots and extended its tracks in anticipation of the hordes of fight fans who would come to Shelby.

Then a problem surfaced. Loy Molumby signed the final contract between the promoters in Shelby and the Dempsey people, stipulating that Dempsey would get *$300,000*—regardless of the outcome of the fight. This extra financial burden convinced Dempsey's manager that all his money might not be forthcoming. So he delayed the fight for weeks, telling the press he wasn't sure whether Dempsey would actually participate in the duel. The result of his noncommittal attitude was a much smaller than expected turnout when the bout did occur. Only twenty thousand people attended, and only eight thousand were required to pay admission.

From a financial standpoint the fight was a disaster. Body Johnson and his father had to make up a loss of $164,500. But from an entertainment standpoint, the match was a big success. The boxers were pretty evenly matched, and neither had an easy contest. There was no knockout. Dempsey won six rounds, and Gibbons won four. Five rounds were even. Dempsey retained his title and walked away with $255,000, while Gibbons received $7,500. The referee was paid $5,000.

Tommy Gibbons visited Shelby many times after the big fight. Jack Dempsey and his manager were never seen or heard in Shelby again.

CHARLIE RUSSELL: COWBOY ARTIST EXTRAORDINAIRE

- 1926 -

THE CIVIL WAR WAS ALMOST OVER and St. Louis was the gateway to the West when Charles Marion Russell was born in nearby Oak Hill in 1864. He was the second son of six children, and his father, Charles Silas, had attended Yale and was a prosperous manufacturer of firebrick.

Although born into a family that valued formal education, young Charlie inherited none of his forebears' respect for "book learning." Instead, two other interests continuously vied for his attention: art and the lure of the West.

Charlie's love of art just seemed to come naturally. By the time he was twelve, he had won a blue ribbon for drawing at the St. Louis County Fair. He may have been smitten with the West because of his grandmother, who was the sister of the famous Bent brothers, Charles and William. These two frontiersmen, with Ceran St. Vrain, had build Bent's Fort on the Arkansas River in the early 1830s. The

Bent brothers' hospitality had soon made the fort a haven for fur trappers, army personnel patroling the Santa Fe Trail, and members of several tribes of southern Plains Indians.

Although young Charlie had already made up his mind to go West and become a cowboy, his parents wanted him to get a formal education. In 1879 they sent him to military school in New Jersey. Constantly at odds with his instructors for failing to keep up with his assignments, Russell returned home after only one year.

When Charlie was almost sixteen, his parents allowed him to make a trip to Montana Territory in the company of a family friend. In March 1880 the two crossed the prairie by train. From the end of the tracks, they took a stage to Helena and then rode horseback to their destination, the Judith Basin.

Charlie Russell fell in love at first sight. When he saw the beauty of the Judith Basin, he knew it was the only place he had any desire to live. He described it like this:

> *Shut off from the outside world, it was a hunter's paradise, bounded by walls of mountains and containing miles of grassy open spaces, more green and beautiful than any man-made parks. These parks and the mountains behind them swarmed with deer, elk, mountain sheep, and bear, besides beaver and other small fur-bearing animals. The creeks were alive with trout.*

After trying his hand at herding sheep, young Russell returned to St. Louis. But he didn't put up with civilization for long. Soon, back in Montana, he became a cowboy, and for the next few years, he worked in the saddle, practicing his drawing, sculpting, and painting whenever he had a little spare time. He often gave his works away to friends and fellow cowboys.

In 1893 he retired from cowpunching to devote himself full-time to art. Although he still painted for fun, he also began to receive commissions, and when he realized how much money he could make doing something he enjoyed, he redoubled his efforts.

Russell's fame grew rapidly. In 1896, at the age of thirty-two, he married eighteen-year-old Nancy Cooper. They shared a happy life together despite their age difference. In fact, Nancy is credited with being an important part of Charlie's success. She dealt shrewdly with potential buyers, often getting prices that flabbergasted Charlie.

Russell's output was prodigious. Scores of oil and watercolor paintings and hundreds of pen and ink sketches adorn the walls of museums and private art collections all over the United States and abroad. Russell's bronzes have rarely been matched for their accuracy in portraying the rough breed of men and the indigenous wildlife of the West.

When Russell died of a heart attack on October 24, 1926, the art world was not alone in mourning. Ranchers, cowboys, Indians, saloon keepers, writers, historians, book and magazine publishers, and newspapermen all realized that they had lost one of their most influential and important friends and spokesmen.

It is said that a man's reputation is best judged by his peers. Charles M. Russell was a man highly regarded by his contemporaries, as well as those who followed him. Someone once asked Andy Adams, author of a popular book on the early cattle industry, what a cowboy of the 1880s looked like. "Ask Charley Russell," he replied. "If he painted a naked cowpuncher swimming across a river, you'd know it was a cowpuncher."

The renowned Texas writer J. Frank Dobie once called Russell "the greatest painter that ever painted a range man, a range cow, a range horse, or a Plains Indian."

Even today, Russell remains one of America's favorite "cowboy artists."

PLENTY COUPS: CHIEF OF THE CROWS

- 1932 -

Of all the Indian chiefs in Montana tribal history, few have commanded more respect than Plenty Coups, one of the last of the great Crow leaders.

The Crows were a sizable tribe of Siouan-speaking people who migrated from the Dakotas to Montana near the end of the eighteenth century. When white explorers and fur traders discovered them, they were living along the Yellowstone and Bighorn Rivers. They called themselves Absaroka, which meant "children of the large-beaked bird."

Margaret Carrington, wife of Colonel Henry Carrington, who built Fort Phil Kearney along the Bozeman Trail, described the Crow country as some of the most beautiful in America. In 1868 she wrote:

> *Partially girt in by the Big Horn and Panther Mountains, yet roaming at will, they were masters of a region of country which has no peer in its exhaustless game*

resources . . . while its natural scenery, made up of snowy crests, pine-clad slopes and summits, crystal waters, and luxuriant vales, certainly has no rival in our great sisterhood of States.

The Crows were constantly at war with their neighbors, particularly the Sioux, Cheyenne, and Blackfeet tribes. But they had a high regard for the trappers and traders who followed Lewis and Clark into the area.

The Crows were a handsome people. George Catlin, the renowned American artist who visited the tribe in the 1830s, described the men as "fine looking, with an ease and grace added to their dignity of manners . . . most of them six feet tall or more . . . and many have cultivated their hair to such an almost incredible length that it sweeps the ground as they walk."

The women were likewise attractive and gifted at making beadwork and tanning leather. They made large tipis from tanned buffalo hides, and, according to Catlin, they "often dress the skins almost as white as linen, and beautifully garnish them with porcupine quills, and paint and ornament them in a variety of ways, as to render them exceedingly picturesque. . . ."

Plenty Coups was born in 1848 near where Billings is today. As a boy he witnessed the last days of the fur trade and the beginning of white immigration into tribal territory. As he reached manhood, he became one of the first of his people to realize that the only way his tribe—or any other—could survive was to adapt quickly to the white man's ways. He spent the rest of his life attempting to lead the Crows peacefully through the transition from buffalo hunters to modern Montanans.

While learning from whites the things he needed to know to save his people from annihilation, Plenty Coups also gave important assistance to U.S. authorities. He furnished Crow scouts for Custer's Sioux expedition in 1876, as well as for the Nez Perce campaign the following year. When the Northern Pacific Railroad considered running its line through parts of Montana, Plenty Coups offered his cooperation.

By 1904 Plenty Coups had become the principal chief of the Crow nation. As a man of obvious influence among his people, he traveled to Washington, D.C., several times and met with high-ranking officials to discuss Indian affairs. When the United States went to war with Germany in 1917, Plenty Coups urged the young men of his nation to take up arms against the Central powers. Although he was almost seventy years old, the amicable chief even volunteered for the army himself.

In 1921 Plenty Coups returned to Washington. This time he served as representative of all Native Americans at the dedication of the Tomb of the Unknown Soldier. The old chief demonstrated his eloquence when he said:

> *For the Indians of America I call upon the Great Spirit of the Red Men with gesture and chant and tribal tongue that the dead should not have died in vain, that war might end, that peace be purchased by the blood of Red Men and White.*

Once, during a visit to Mount Vernon, Plenty Coups decided he would like his home, like George Washington's, to be memorialized as a lasting shrine and museum to his people. When he died in 1932, his wishes were observed, and today the Chief Plenty Coups Memorial State Monument stands near Pryor, a tribute to this remarkable Indian statesman.

SMOKEJUMPERS TO THE RESCUE

- 1939 -

In the summer of 1988, millions of Americans watched as the magic of television brought the devastating Yellowstone National Park fires into their living rooms. Before the flames were extinguished, they devoured about 1.4 million acres of prime forestland in the states of Wyoming, Montana, and Idaho. Firefighters from many states battled those flames from June through mid-September.

Among the unsung heroes of the drama were the Forest Service smokejumpers. These brave men and women, who operate out of Missoula and several other bases throughout the West, are called upon hundreds of times each year to travel all over the country and contribute their special firefighting skills to protect the nation's forests and parks.

Smokejumping had its official beginnings in the United States in 1939, when funds were authorized for an experiment combining parachute jumping with firefighting. Professional parachute riggers and jumpers employed by the Eagle Parachute Company of

Lancaster, Pennsylvania, were hired to participate in theproject. From October 5 through November 15, 1939, they made a series of jumps into the Chelan National Forest in Washington to assess the value of parachuting into remote areas to combat wildfire.

Before the experiments were over, Forest Service firefighters also made several jumps into the targeted area. The experimenters concluded that smokejumpers could successfully jump into wilderness areas with enough gear to contribute significantly to a ground-based firefighting effort.

In 1940 Major William Cary Lee visited the smokejumping facilities in Missoula to study the techniques that had been developed by the Forest Service. Lee used the knowledge he gained in Montana to help develop a training program for army airborne troops. During World War II, Lee commanded the famed 101st Airborne Division and later served as the first chief of the U.S. Airborne Command.

During the summer of 1949, one of the worst fires in Montana history ignited the Helena National Forest. The area had gone several weeks without rain, and when fire struck, it spread quickly. Sixteen smokejumpers from the Missoula base parachuted into the blaze around four in the afternoon of August 5. They landed safely and were preparing to go to work when the fire raged out of control, killing thirteen of them.

The great fire of 1949 became known as the Mann Gulch Fire, and the following year moviemakers from Hollywood visited Missoula to make a film about the horrible episode. Released in 1952 by Twentieth Century Fox, the movie was called *Red Skies of Montana.* It starred Richard Widmark, Jeffrey Hunter, and Richard Boone.

Over the years smokejumping equipment and airplanes have become more sophisticated. In the early days a jumper typically carried a thirty-foot parachute and a twenty-seven-foot reserve. He wore a regular football helmet equipped with a wire-mesh face mask.

Heavy logger boots and a protective, felt-padded suit completed his uniform. He usually jumped from a Ford Trimotor or a Curtis Travelair airplane.

Today, the jumper's chute is maneuverable, and the jumper can alter his rate of descent. Clothing and other equipment have become lighter and more durable, and the jumpsuit itself is now fireproof. Several airplane models have been used, including DC-3s, C-47s, and Cessna 206s.

By 1990 about four hundred smokejumpers were on duty across the nation. In the half century since their debut, they have made close to 350,000 jumps. The men and women of the Forest Service's parachute brigade stand ready to fly at a moment's notice to anywhere in the country where wildfire burns out of control.

FROM MONTANA TO HOLLYWOOD

- 1941 -

MONTANA HAD BEEN A STATE FOR ONLY twelve years when Frank James Cooper was born in Helena on May 7, 1901. A quiet, almost shy youth, Cooper loved art and aspired to be a cartoonist.

As a young man Cooper went to Hollywood, where he got a job as an extra in a silent movie entitled *Lightning Justice.* Impressed by what they saw in this tall, laconic Westerner, several directors vied for his talent. In 1926 he appeared in his first leading role under the name he would use for the rest of his life, Gary Cooper. His success in this movie, *The Winning of Barbara Worth,* ensured his future as a movie star.

When Owen Wister's *The Virginian,* considered by some to be the first Western novel, was made into a talking movie in 1929, Cooper was the perfect actor for the title role. Who else but quiet, unassuming Cooper could have galvanized the audience with that unforgettable line, "When you call me that, smile!"

With the success of *The Virginian,* Hollywood had found its Western star. One critic has written that "during the 1930s and 1940s his decent backwoods heroes spoke up for the values and standards of small-town rural America in direct opposition to the gabby, big-city wise guys represented by James Cagney, Edward G. Robinson, and Humphrey Bogart." It was one such "backwoods hero" who catapulted Cooper to international fame. *Sergeant York,* based on the life of Alvin C. York, the World War I Medal of Honor winner from rural Tennessee, won Cooper his first Academy Award in 1941.

As his role in *Sergeant York* proved, Cooper's talents went beyond Westerns. Over the next few years, the man from Helena played such widely diverse roles as the expatriate soldier in Ernest Hemingway's *For Whom the Bell Tolls,* the British hero in *Lives of a Bengal Lancer,* and the peaceable farmer in *Friendly Persuasion.*

But Cooper was best known for his Westerns. One role followed another: *Vera Cruz, They Came to Cordura, High Noon,* and *The Hanging Tree.* He won his second Oscar in 1952 for his role in *High Noon* as the sheriff torn between love for his new bride and duty to protect his town against outlaws.

Myrna Loy, another film idol of the 1930s, 1940s, and 1950s, also hailed from Big Sky Country. A third-generation Montanan, she was born Myrna Adele Williams on August 2, 1905, in Radersburg. When she was five, her family moved to Helena, where Myrna grew up not far from Cooper's home.

Myrna's theatrical talent showed up early. In 1917 the Montana *Record-Herald* reported that "Miss Myrna Williams . . . gave the feature, 'The Bluebird Dance,' in the Rose Dream Operetta, presented at the Marlow Theater last week." Myrna had not only designed her own gown for the play but had choreographed her dance sequence as well.

In Hollywood Myrna changed her name to Myrna Loy and became a household word during the 1930s and 1940s for her portrayal of Nora Charles in the many *Thin Man* movies, costarring William Powell. In a poll of twenty million moviegoers, she was named "Queen of the Movies," and women all over America underwent plastic surgery in hopes of copying Loy's famous upturned nose. The beauty from Montana was courted by some of Hollywood's leading men of the times, including John Barrymore, Clark Gable, Spencer Tracy, and Leslie Howard.

Aside from her *Thin Man* roles, Loy starred in such movies as the original *Ben Hur, The Desert Song, The Great Ziegfeld, The Best Years of Our Lives,* and *Cheaper by the Dozen.* Despite Loy's acting ability and long-term popularity, she was never nominated for an Academy Award, but she was honored in 1985 by the Academy of Motion Picture Arts and Sciences at Carnegie Hall.

Actors are not the only Montanans to whom Hollywood owes homage. Prolific writer Dorothy M. Johnson penned short stories that were eventually made into successful motion pictures. *The Hanging Tree* starred fellow Montanan Gary Cooper; *The Man Who Shot Liberty Valance* saw John Wayne and Jimmy Stewart in its lead roles; and *A Man Called Horse* starred Richard Harris.

A. B. Guthrie, Jr., wrote the book *The Big Sky,* which was made into a movie of the same name starring Kirk Douglas. Guthrie also wrote the Academy Award–nominated screenplay to the movie *Shane,* as well as that for *The Kentuckian,* featuring Burt Lancaster.

JEANNETTE RANKIN: A DOVE IN CONGRESS

- 1941 -

It was Good Friday, April 6, 1917, and Jeannette Rankin sat nervously in her seat on the Republican side of the U.S. House of Representatives. Clad in a plain blue dress and without her usual broad-brimmed hat, the thirty-six-year-old Missoula native was about to cast her vote on a resolution declaring war with Germany. If the resolution passed, it would toss the United States into the midst of the deadly world war that was raging in Europe.

The problem was, Rankin didn't know which way to vote. As the first woman ever elected to the House of Representatives, she had the support of women's groups everywhere. She was a self-declared pacifist, and her views on war were widely known. So why this uncertainty?

One reason for her exasperation was that some of the nation's women's groups were prowar, while others were antiwar. Although most women agreed on such issues as women's and children's rights and labor matters, there was no neat consensus among them on the issue of war. Some of her most rabid supporters believed that voting against the war would dash her hopes of reelection and thereby harm the women's movement in the United States.

When the clerk called her name during the first roll call, Rankin remained silent. A deadly hush fell over the House chambers. The clerk continued the roll. Representative Joe Cannon, an old veteran from Illinois, reportedly approached Rankin and said, "Little woman, you cannot afford not to vote. You represent the womanhood of the country in the American Congress. I shall not advise you how to vote, but you should vote one way or the other, as your conscience dictates."

The tension mounted. The second roll call began. When Rankin's name was called, she paused and then declared, "I want to stand by my country, but I cannot vote for war."

Reactions were mixed. Some members of the House and the public were elated that Rankin had stood firm by her antiwar convictions and voted her heart. Others blasted her for being soft on Germany, a publicity seeker, and not worthy of public office, although fifty-five other members of Congress had also voted against the war resolution.

In late 1917, when another war resolution was considered, this time against Austria-Hungary, Rankin voted for it. Defending her stance on the basis that this resolution was a "mere technicality in the prosecution of a war already declared," she let it be known that her pacifist beliefs had not changed.

> *I still believe war is a stupid and futile way of attempting to settle international difficulties. I believe war can be avoided and will be avoided when the people, the men and women in America, as well as in Germany,*

have the controlling voice in their government. Today special interests are controlling the world.

As some of her women's rights associates had predicted, Rankin was decisively defeated in the next election. She moved to Georgia, where she continued to lobby for peace and for women's and children's rights. In the spring of 1940, shortly before her sixtieth birthday, she returned to her native Montana. After a few months of testing the political waters, she decided to run again for Congress. Campaigning under the slogan "Prepare to the limit for defense, keep our men out of Europe," she barely survived the primary and then won the general election.

Rankin cast a second vote that would stand out in history on December 8, 1941, only hours after the Japanese attacked the U.S. naval base at Pearl Harbor. During the congressional debates that day, Rankin tried desperately to speak to the assembled lawmakers, but she was repeatedly denied the floor. The roll call began, and when Rankin's name was called, she quietly replied, "As a woman, I can't go to war and I refuse to send anyone else."

This vote differed from the one she'd cast during World War I. In 1917 Rankin had been one of many to vote against American participation in the conflict. This time she was the lone dissenter. When the roll call was completed, the final tally of both houses was 470 for war and 1 against.

Rankin's world erupted in pandemonium. The public viewed her vote as nothing short of treason, and she had to be escorted from the House to her office by Capitol police. Her own brother angrily told her, "Montana is 110 percent against you."

After finishing her term in 1942, Rankin returned to Georgia but remained active in antiwar protests throughout the Vietnam conflict. The nation's first female representative died in 1973, just short of her ninety-third birthday.

WILL JAMES: MONTANA'S MYSTERY MAN

- 1942 -

WHEN WILL JAMES DIED in Hollywood in 1942 from "alcoholic complications," he was as much a mystery as when he'd arrived in Montana in 1910. Only fifty years old at the time of his death, James had achieved recognition across the country as an author and artist. But his modest fame was built on a past that was almost entirely fiction.

James was born in Quebec to French-Canadian parents and was christened Joseph Ernest Nephtali Dufault. He apparently left his parents' home in Montreal when he was about fifteen years old and headed for the Canadian West. Around 1910 he appeared in Montana using the name Will James.

Why James wanted to keep his past a secret will probably never be known. Whatever the reason, he persisted throughout his life in portraying himself as a Montana-born cowboy whose father was from West Texas and whose mother was a Southern Californian. He told the story of his fictitious beginnings in *Lone Cowboy,* an "autobiograpy" published in 1930 after he had attained a fair degree of fame as a writer and artist. Perhaps he was afraid his real origins would diminish the cowboy image so popular with his loyal followers.

In *Lone Cowboy* James wrote that he was orphaned at an early age and adopted by a woodsman named Jean Baupre. When Will was fourteen, old Baupre died, and once again the young cowboy had to fend for himself.

In reality James worked for several Montana ranches as a cowboy, traveled to Nevada to break wild horses, followed the rodeo circuit for a while, and spent some time in Hollywood doing stunts for the new Western movies that were being cranked out by the studios.

In 1914, during his stay in Nevada, James was arrested for cattle rustling. He was sentenced to the state prison at Carson City but was paroled a couple of years later. He served in the Twenty-First Infantry during World War I but was on active duty for less than a year.

Throughout his rambling days James was a prolific sketcher of horses, cattle, and cowboy scenes. When a rodeo accident forced him to spend some time off in 1919, he decided to give up bronc busting and become an artist.

A passage in *Lone Cowboy* provides a glimpse of James's almost comical belief in his own abilities. According to his own story, he visited Charlie Russell, who was at the peak of his popularity.

> *I picked up the little bunch of drawings I brought with me and begins strutting towards the artist's place. . . . My eyes roamed over them paintings and the more I looked at 'em the more I admired 'em, and then I begin to lose hope. I could never be an artist half as good as him, I thought. After a while the artist himself*

> *came in . . . and I felt mighty insignificant as I stood up to meet him. . . . I gawked around the place and then turned to the artist. He'd went to work on the half finished picture like as if I wasn't around. . . . Finally he layed his brush down and begin looking thru my little pencil drawings. . . . It was then I reared back and grinned to myself in expecting a look of surprise, hearing compliments and then being told of a way where I could sudden make a gunnysack full of money before sundown. . . . I was grinning right along and sort of proud as the artist shuffled my drawings. . . . When I asked him what I should do with 'em, and where I could sell 'em, he explained . . ., "Just scatter 'em around in saloons. . . . Somebody might buy 'em."*

James enrolled in the California School of Fine Arts in San Francisco and began to take his art seriously. Maynard Dixon, already nationally recognized for his murals of southwestern scenes and his magazine illustrations, suggested that James quit his formal schooling and become a full-time artist. And so, in the January 1920 issue of *Sunset* magazine, James's cowboy art was first published.

A short time later, James combined his artistic and writing talents to produce a magazine article entitled, "Bucking Horses and Bucking Horse Riders," which he sold to *Scribner's Magazine* for $300, a lot of money in those days. With this major conquest James's future as a writer and cowboy artist was assured.

In addition to *Lone Cowboy,* James wrote *Smoky the Cowhorse, The Drifting Cowboy, All in the Day's Riding, Cowboys North and South, Cow Country* and many others. In 1928 he bought a twelve-thousand-acre cattle ranch near Billings where he did most of his later writing, painting, and drawing.

When asked about his profession, the happy-go-lucky James once commented, "I just write till I'm tired an' then spell off 'nd draw till I get tired of that."

THE KILLER QUAKE

- 1959 -

In August 1959 Irving Witkind, a geologist with the U.S. Geological Survey, was camped with fellow scientist J. B. Epstein on an overlook above Hebgen Lake, in the Madison River Canyon. Witkind and Epstein had spent the summer surveying and documenting the rock strata in this particular part of southwestern Montana.

The night of August 17 started quietly. Across the river a full moon cast long shadows below the giant trees lining Hebgen Lake. All the campgrounds around the lake were full of visitors wanting to breathe in the beauty of the surrounding wilderness. By eleven o'clock, almost everyone had retired, and a deathlike peace settled over the valley.

At 11:37 Witkind and Epstein's trailer began to shake violently, jolting them from sleep. At first they thought the vehicle had somehow fallen off its jacks and was speeding downhill. Witkind jumped out to investigate and discovered that the trailer was motionless, but the ground and the canyon walls were swaying back and forth. Trees thrashed furiously, and yet there was no wind.

With his training in geology, it didn't take Witkind long to realize he was standing in the midst of an earthquake—something he'd only been able to study in textbooks before. Now a major temblor was buckling the ground beneath his very feet.

The two geologists were luckier than many of the vacationers sleeping in the canyon. When the quake finally ended, twenty-eight men, women, and children were dead.

Hebgen Dam and Hebgen Lake dropped ten feet during the first tremor, which is estimated to have lasted from five seconds to two minutes. The concrete core of the dam was cracked in four places. While the dam didn't break, it was severely damaged.

Meanwhile, downstream from Hebgen Dam, a section of the south valley wall caved in, dumping thirty-eight million cubic yards of rock and debris into the Madison River. The natural dam formed by the slide was about a mile long and three-quarters of a mile wide. The lake formed behind the dam was appropriately named Earthquake Lake.

Five days after the earthquake, a flow of earth that had previously stabilized began to move again. It was situated along Kirkwood Creek, northeast of Hebgen Lake. Local firefighters, who had been sent into the area to combat a small blaze, reported that the earth moved and groaned beneath them.

The Hebgen earthquake originally measured 7.1 on the Richter scale, but it was later upgraded to 7.5. Groundwater levels fluctuated throughout the United States. Even in Hawaii some thirty-two hundred miles away, the water level in local wells fluctuated by almost an inch and a half.

The region around Hebgen Lake and the Madison River Canyon is now quiet once again. The scars in the forests have partially healed, and the waters of the streams run fresh and clear again. One year after the disastrous quake, the Madison River Earthquake Area was dedicated. A bronze plaque memorializes the unfortunate victims of that tragic night in 1959.

THE WILD HORSES OF THE PRYOR MOUNTAINS

- 1969 -

In the Pryor Mountains along the sparsely populated Montana–Wyoming border, wild horses roam free, a romantic remnant of the distant past. Although domestic stock that has escaped or been released into the wilds has helped to propagate these herds, the animals are direct descendents of those brought to Mexico by Spanish explorer Hernando Cortes in 1519.

In 1964 the Bureau of Land Management announced that it would round up and sell at auction the two hundred or so wild horses roaming the Pryor Mountains. Area ranchers and the townspeople of nearby Lovell, Wyoming, were upset by the arbitrary proposal. They had always considered the wild horses an endangered part of their western heritage. The animals deserved better than ending up as dog food, they argued.

And so proponents and opponents of the horse herds began a propaganda war. Opponents argued that the local herds had only recently gone wild, that they were remnants of domestic stock mixed with some army horses that had purposely been set free to strengthen the herds' genetic makeup. Proponents worked to prove the historical significance of the animals. For proof they submitted recently discovered skeletal remains from the area showing that the spines of some of the wild horses had one less vertebra than those of modern horses—a distinguishing trait of the Spanish mustang.

Years of lawsuits, meetings, telephone calls, and trips back and forth to Washington, D.C., followed as supporters of the wild horses worked feverishly to keep them safe from roundup. Finally, in 1969, Secretary of the Interior Stewart Udall learned about the BLM's five-year-old plan to exterminate the Montana horse herd. He terminated it and designated the entire region of several thousand acres the Pryor Mountain Wild Horse Refuge. Montana's senior senator, Mike Mansfield, was so elated that he had the BLM directive to scrap the plan published in the Congressional Record for September 12, 1969.

A visit to the Pryor Mountain Wild Horse Refuge is an unforgettable experience. The best way to see the wild horses is to park the car and strike out on foot across the dry tableland. Tipi rings made hundreds of years ago can be seen here and there. In the hot summer the horses gather in the shade of the trees that clump on the horizon. The sight of a wild stallion racing across the coulees is like a special gift from the past.

THE CENTENNIAL CATTLE DRIVE

- 1989 -

AS THE ONE-HUNDREDTH ANNIVERSARY OF STATEHOOD approached in 1989, a group of Montana residents searched for a way to celebrate that would fittingly reflect the heritage of the Big Sky. They decided to stage a gigantic cattle drive in the image of those that crossed the open range a century before.

At the forefront of the plan were Jim Wempner, a local rancher, and Stan Lynde and Barry McWilliams, both cowboy cartoonists. Their biggest obstacle was civilization and its attendant highways, fences, transmission lines, and private land ownership. Persistently, the trio plotted a sixty-mile route from Roundup through the Bull Mountains to Billings. The drive would take six days.

On Labor Day 1989 the big roundup began. Local residents and ranchers paid a $40 fee and one cow to participate. The cattle were later auctioned off, and part of the proceeds was donated to the Montana Rural Development Fund.

People flocked from across the country to take part in the big event. Television magnate Ted Turner, astronaut Jim Adamson, and

Montana Senator Conrad Burns all joined in, as did more than three thousand cowboys and cowgirls. The youngest rider was 5 and the oldest was 102. There were more than 2,800 cattle and 208 covered wagons involved.

The cattle drive was an appropriate way to celebrate Montana's entry into the union in 1889. Ever since the first Texans began herding tens of thousands of cattle north into Montana, the livestock business has been one of the state's most lucrative industries.

Although the cattle drive was a spectacular event, it paled in comparison to the impact of statehood. Montanans tried twice to gain statehood after their territory was created in 1864, but both times their pleas were rejected. The first try in 1866 failed because Montana didn't have enough population. The second failure in 1884 was due to party politics. The Republicans controlled the U.S. Senate, while the Democrats held sway in the House of Representatives and the White House. Unwilling to upset the delicate balance between the two parties by admitting new states, Congress simply deferred action.

In the election of 1888, the Republican Party gained control of both houses of Congress, as well as the presidency. In February 1889 the governments of the Dakotas, Washington, and Montana were advised that statehood would be granted once they drew up proper state constitutions.

On October 1, 1889, Montana voters approved their new state constitution. The vote was 24,676 for adoption and 2,274 against. Federal approval followed shortly, and on November 8, 1889, Montana became the forty-first state in the union.

The state of Montana got off to a rocky start. The state legislature was evenly divided between Democrats and Republicans. Democrat Joseph K. Toole was elected the first governor, and Republican Thomas Carter was sent to Washington as Montana's first congressman. The legislature, unable to reach a compromise between the two parties, elected four U.S. senators: Republicans Wilbur Fisk Sanders and T. C. Power and Democrats W. A. Clark and Martin Maginnis. The U.S. Senate had to choose whom to seat. Made up mostly of Republicans, it selected the two Republicans.

Within nine months, six new states were admitted to the United States: Montana, Wyoming, Washington, North and South Dakota, and Idaho. The amount of territory gained by the Union was nearly 550,000 square miles, more than four times the area of the original thirteen states.

Participants in the Cattle Drive of 1989 got a special sense of that geographic grandeur as they trailed herd under the Big Sky.

A. B. GUTHRIE: LITERARY GIANT

- 1991 -

A. B. "BUD" GUTHRIE, JR., WAS ON ASSIGNMENT for *Holiday* magazine. Trying to track down a piece of information for the article he was writing, he called a former associate at *The Leader,* the Lexington, Kentucky, newspaper from which he'd recently retired.

"Congratulations, Bud!" the old colleague exclaimed as soon as he realized who was calling. A startled Guthrie asked what for.

"You've won the Pulitzer Prize. Just came in on the wire," was the reply.

In his autobiography, *The Blue Hen's Chick,* Guthrie recalled that about forty-five minutes after the surprising conversation, he received official notification that he'd won the 1950 Pulitzer for fiction for his novel *The Way West.*

Guthrie was born in 1901 in Bedford, Indiana. The same year, his father moved the family to Choteau, Montana, where the elder Guthrie became the first principal of the Teton County Free High School.

Young Guthrie was educated locally and then attended college for one year at the University of Washington in Seattle. Suffering from homesickness, he transferred to the University of Montana, where he majored in journalism. In July 1926 Guthrie went back East, this time to Lexington, Kentucky, where his uncle had promised him a job as a cub reporter with the town's daily newspaper.

Guthrie spent the next twenty-one years with *The Leader,* serving in a variety of positions. During his tenure at the newspaper, he was awarded a Nieman fellowship to Harvard, and while there he rubbed elbows with some of the nation's most successful journalists. He returned to Kentucky with a renewed resolve to write another novel, an idea that had intrigued him for some time. His first try at fiction writing had already resulted in a disappointing book entitled, *Murders at Moon Dance,* published in 1943.

Back in Lexington Guthrie spent most of his spare time working on a manuscript that he'd been nurturing for several years. Upon completion he sold it to William Sloan Associates of New York. The book was published in 1947 as *The Big Sky,* and it was a bold, magnificent work about mountain men and Indians during the great days of the Rocky Mountain fur trade. Picked up immediately by the Book of the Month Club, *The Big Sky* assured Guthrie of the financial means he needed to continue his writing of quality historical fiction about the American West.

After *The Big Sky* came *The Way West,* about the migration along the Oregon Trail. *These Thousand Hills,* the last of his trilogy on America's western movement, focused on the settlement of Montana.

Guthrie's literary success brought him instant recognition. He received an honorary doctor of literature degree from his alma mater, the University of Montana. In Lexington he taught creative writing at the University of Kentucky for five years. And then, out of the blue, he received an invitation from Hollywood to come to the West

Coast and write screenplays. Howard Hawks had recently bought the screen rights to *The Big Sky,* and, impressed by Guthrie's use of dialogue, he'd recommended Guthrie to producer-director George Stevens.

Guthrie's first job was to write the script for the epic Western *Shane,* by Jack Schaefer. The movie starred Alan Ladd, Van Heflin, Jean Arthur, Brandon De Wilde, Ben Johnson, and a young actor named Walter Jack Palance, who played the hired gunfighter. *Shane* won immediate praise, along with six Academy Award nominations. Later came *The Kentuckian,* featuring Burt Lancaster and based on the novel *The Gabriel Horn.* In the meantime Guthrie's *The Big Sky* was made into an epic movie starring Kirk Douglas.

In 1953 Guthrie and his family returned to Montana, where they divided their time between a vacation home west of Choteau and a home in Great Falls. He served as the general editor for McGraw-Hill's American Trails series and wrote a few articles for magazines. But mostly he enjoyed the people and countryside of his beloved Montana.

Guthrie died on April 26, 1991, at his home near Choteau. In an interview he once said, "I don't . . . promote the myth of the Old West. . . . I want to talk about real people in real times." That philosophy made him one of this generation's finest novelists and portrayers of the American West.

THE CAPTURE OF THE UNABOMBER

- 1996 -

As they awoke on the morning of April 3, 1996, not one of Lincoln's five hundred residents could possibly have known what was in store for their small Montana town. Snuggled in the vast Helena National Forest west of the Continental Divide, the village had once enjoyed the profits of a thriving mining industry, but now most livings were being made from timber and tourism. Due to the area's remoteness, back in the early 1970s one could purchase land there cheaply yet still be close to some of Montana's larger towns, including Great Falls, Missoula, and Helena.

Ted Kaczynski recognized a value when he saw one. In 1971 this native of Chicago, in partnership with his brother, David, purchased a 1.4 acre plot in Florence Gulch along Stemple Pass Road southeast of Lincoln. Kaczynski, who had an undergraduate degree from Harvard and a master's and a PhD from the University of Michigan, and who had most recently taught mathematics at the University of California at Berkeley, was surely one of Lincoln's better-educated immigrants. He soon built a primitive twelve-foot-by-ten-foot frame cabin on his small parcel of ground and began a life of solitude. His abode had no electricity or water, and its sole source of heat was a wood-burning stove. He drove an old automobile and later swapped it for a decrepit pickup truck, but when the pickup died, he relied on his bicycle or his own feet for traveling. For months on end he was seldom seen by anyone, except when he passed a neighbor's house on one of his rare trips to town. He grew his own vegetables, including potatoes, carrots, and onions, and took to the thick forests to hunt wild game for meat. For all intents and purposes, he was a latter-day mountain man.

Kaczynski lived outside of Lincoln for years without attracting undue attention. Most of the town's residents who had met or talked to him just figured he was a hermit who would rather spend time alone than socialize with his neighbors. But after Kaczynski moved into the neighborhood, bizarre events began to occur, including the killing of a number of dogs, the destruction of some heavy machinery, vandalism of several cabins and logging equipment, and shots fired into buildings. But no one ever suspected that the hermit from Florence Gulch could have had anything to do with these unsettling incidents.

Kaczynski had been a resident of the Lincoln area for seven years when, in May 1978, newspapers across the country carried a story describing how a security guard at Northwestern University had been injured after opening a package he'd found in a parking lot. Inside the parcel was what appeared to be a homemade bomb. One year later, a Northwestern University student was hurt by a similar bomb, and that incident was followed in November by an explosion in the cargo area of an American Airlines jet that forced it to make an emergency landing at Dulles International Airport in Washington, D.C. After the president of United Airlines was injured by a similar bomb at his Chicago home on June 10, 1980, a task force was assembled to get to the bottom of these bizarre bombings. The task force soon dubbed the perpetrator the "Unabomber," with the "Un" standing for "university" and the "a" denoting "airlines"—the terrorist's two most obvious targets.

For the next fifteen years, while authorities fruitlessly pursued the case, the Unabomber continued to strike at will. Bombings occurred in places as widely separated as the University of California at Berkeley, Vanderbilt University in Nashville, Salt Lake City, Sacramento, Yale University, and the University of Michigan. During his extended spree of violence, the serial bomber seemed to be targeting university research laboratories, airlines, and hi-tech industries, killing three people and injuring twenty-three others. Task force investigators could only shake their heads. It appeared that the Unabomber might never be captured.

Although some Lincoln residents had noticed, in the days before April 3, 1996, a few new faces driving strange automobiles around the area, no great amount of thought was given to these sightings until the fateful morning when the Unabomber was captured. Federal authorities, tipped off by Kaczynski's brother, David, had approached the bomber's cabin and, after luring him outside, arrested him and hauled him off to the Lewis and Clark County jail for questioning.

David had become suspicious that his brother might be the notorious Unabomber after reading the so-called "Unabomber Manifesto," published in the September 19, 1995, issue of the *Washington Post.* David Kaczynski saw in the document remarkable similarities to some of his brother's earlier writings.

Ted Kaczynski was eventually sent to Sacramento to stand trial. After his arrest his "secret" cabin was discovered, located even deeper in the wilderness. Searchers found bomb-making supplies, survival gear, and hundreds of pages of documents written by the Unabomber.

Before the investigation was over, more than twenty-two thousand pages of notes were located. They filled scores of three-ring binders, small notebooks, and scratch pads and documented Kaczynski's adult life up until he was arrested.

The documents revealed that the Unabomber was a deranged man, one who hated society and had a tremendous distrust for advanced technology. "I often became terribly angry at someone, or hated someone, but as a matter of prudence, I could not express that anger or hatred openly," he once wrote. On another occasion, he added, "The technological society may be in some sense inevitable, but it is so only because of the way people behave." He also wrote, "I hate people . . . but the main reason is that people are responsible for the technological society and its associated phenomena, from motorcycles to computers to psychological controls. . . ." He later added, "Of course, the people I hate most are those who consciously and willfully promote the technological society, such as scientists, big businessmen, union leaders, politicians, etc., etc."

In Sacramento Kaczynski was charged with a plethora of crimes, including bomb manufacture and transportation resulting in death and injury, and carrying a firearm while committing a crime. On January 22, 1998, just as jury selection was winding down, the bomber's attorneys worked out a deal with federal prosecutors that sentenced him to serve several life sentences in prison with no possibility of parole. He was also ordered to pay restitution of more than $15 million to his victims and their families. His fate was read by the judge on May 4, and the man who had eluded authorities for eighteen years was hustled off to a maximum security prison.

MONTANA FACTS & TRIVIA

Montana is the fourth largest state in the nation after Alaska, Texas, and California. It encompasses 147,138 square miles, or almost ninety-five million acres. It averages 550 miles from east to west and 275 from north to south.

The mean elevation of Montana is 3,400 feet. The highest point in the state is Granite Peak in Park County, with an altitude of 12,799 feet. The lowest point is along the Kootenai River in Lincoln County, at an altitude of 1,800 feet.

The geographical center of Montana is eleven miles west of Lewistown.

The latest agricultural statistics show that Montana contains approximately 27,870 farms totaling about 59,612,403 acres, an average of 2,139 acres per farm.

The 2000 Census revealed that Montana had a population of 902,195 people. The 2005 estimated population was 935,670, placing Montana forty-fourth in the nation in terms of population.

The coldest temperature ever recorded in Montana was seventy degrees Fahrenheit below zero on January 20, 1954, at Rogers Pass, west of Great Falls.

The hottest temperature was 117 degrees on July 5, 1937, at Medicine Lake in the northeast corner of the state.

The record maximum precipitation within a twenty-four-hour period was 11.5 inches of rain, measured at the Circle Weather Station on June 20, 1921.

Montana became a U.S. territory in 1864. It became the forty-first state on November 8, 1889.

The capital of Montana is Helena, with a 2003 estimated population of 26,718.

The largest city in Montana is Billings, with a 2003 estimated population of 95,220.

Montana contains fifty-six counties.

The word "Montana" is Spanish for "mountainous."

The state motto is *Oro y Plata,* meaning "Gold and Silver."

Montana's official state nickname is "The Treasure State." It is also commonly called "Big Sky Country."

The state bird is the western meadowlark *(Sturnella neglecta)*, the state mammal is the grizzly bear *(Ursus arctos horribilis)*, and the state fish is the blackspotted cutthroat trout *(Salmo clarki)*.

The state flower is the bitterroot *(Lewisia rediviva),* and the state tree is the ponderosa pine *(Pinus ponderosa).*

The unofficial state song is *Montana.*

The state flag is a dark blue banner with the state seal in the center. The seal depicts a plow, pick, and shovel beside a river in the mountains.

FOR FURTHER READING

Bradshaw, Glenda Kaye, Robert H. Fletcher, and Jon Axline. *Montana's Historical Highway Markers.* Helena: Montana Historical Society Press, 1999.

Conklin, Dave. *Montana History Weekends: 52 Adventures in History.* Guilford, CT: Globe Pequot Press, 2002.

Dimsdale, Thomas J. *The Vigilantes of Montana.* Helena: Globe Pequot Press, 2003.

Fritz, Harry W., Mary Murphy and Robert R. Swartout. *Montana Legacy: Essays on History, People, and Place.* Helena: Montana Historical Society Press, 2002.

Johanek, Durrae and John. *Montana Folks.* Helena: Globe Pequot Press, 2004.

Morrison, John, and Catherine Wright Morrison. Mavericks: *The Lives and Battles of Montana's Political Legends.* Helena: Montana Historical Society Press, 2003.

Shirley, Gayle C. *More than Petticoats: Remarkable Montana Women.* Helena: Globe Pequot Press, 1995.

Smith, Norma. *Jeannette Rankin, America's Conscience.* Helena: Montana Historical Society Press, 2002.

Swibold, Dennis L. *Copper Chorus: Mining, Politics, and the Montana Press, 1889-1959.* Helena: Montana Historical Society Press, 2006.

Thompson, Francis M. *A Tenderfoot in Montana: Reminiscences of the Gold Rush, the Vigilantes, and the Birth of Montana Territory.* Helena: Montana Historical Society Press, 2004.

Van West, Carroll. *Traveler's Companion to Montana History.* Helena: Montana Historical Society Press, 1986.

Wilson, Gary A. *Outlaw Tales of Montana, Second Edition.* Helena: Globe Pequot Press, 2003.

INDEX

ABOUT THE AUTHOR

Jim Crutchfield is a historian and writer with more than thirteen books and hundreds of magazine articles to his credit. He is a member of the Western Writers of America, National Cowboy Hall of Fame, Lewis and Clark Trail Heritage Foundation, and numerous other historical organizations. Crutchfield frequently writes about mountain men, including his book *A Primer of the North American Fur Trade;* western expansion and settlement; and his native Tennessee.